D0718826

Making Work
Experience Count

Making Work Experience Count

How to get the right work experience and improve your career prospects

SALLY LONGSON
2nd edition

How To Books

Published by How To Books Ltd,
3 Newtec Place, Magdalen Road,
Oxford OX4 1RE. United Kingdom.
Tel: (01865) 793806. Fax: (01865) 248780.
email: info@howtobooks.co.uk
http://www.howtobooks.co.uk

Second edition 1999

British Library Cataloguing in Publication Data.
A catalogue record for this book is available from
the British Library.

Cover design by Shireen Nathoo Design
Cover copy Sallyann Sheridan
Cover image PhotoDisc
Cartoons by Mike Flanagan

Produced for How To Books by Deer Park Productions
Typeset by PDQ Typesetting, Newcastle-under-Lyme, Staffs.
Printed and bound by Cromwell Press, Trowbridge, Wiltshire

NOTE: The material contained in this book is set out in good
faith for general guidance and no liability can be accepted
for loss or expense incurred as a result of relying in particular
circumstances on statements made in the book. Laws and
regulations are complex and liable to change, and readers should
check the current position with the relevant authorities before
making personal arrangements.

Contents

List of Illustrations

Preface
to the second edition

Work experience can be a powerful aid in your search for the right career with the right company. It helps you to focus on your skills and personal development, and to decide where you might fit into the workplace. In today's competitive job market, you need to know what your skills, strengths and interests are, and how to market those well, if you are to get the job you want. Treat work experience as an investment and analyse your returns carefully. And keep building on your experience and skills, even when you're in work. This edition has a new chapter, with tips on how you can do this at work and in your spare time.

Work experience puts you in the heart of an organisation, where your efforts will be appreciated and noted. A qualification alone isn't enough to get a job any more. Work experience on a CV or application form stands out, expecially if you describe what you've learned as a result of it. It makes a selector sit up and think, 'I want to find out more about this person – let's call him in for an interview.'

Many people get their first job offer through work experience. Why? *Because they made the effort to do it and proved their worth.* They're tried and tested in an employer's world. They've proved their commitment and interest, and they know what they're letting themselves in for. Employers feel more comfortable taking them on.

The terminology 'his' or 'her' has been used throughout this book without any sexual discrimination intended.

I would like to thank everybody at How To Books for their enthusiasm and support for this book and my family for their interest, and in particular my husband, Paul, for all his encouragement.

Sally Longson

11

1

Understanding Work Experience

ASKING WHAT EXPERIENCE YOU HAVE HAD

If there's one question employers ask that's guaranteed to make newcomers or returners to the job market mad, it's about what experience you have had. 'How can I get experience if you don't give me the opportunity?' you feel like answering. In the back of your mind you may hear yourself saying:

- 'Everyone has to start somewhere – just give me the chance.'
- 'How do you expect me to have experience if this is my first job?'
- 'Give me the job and I'll soon have experience.'
- 'How am I supposed to get experience if no one will give me a job?'

Do any of these sound familiar? Can you feel the frustration when the employer asks what relevant experience you have had or when you see that advert stating 'experience preferred'? This book will show you ways to get that experience and those skills which employers want – and how to make them count.

GETTING A STRATEGIC ADVANTAGE

People at all levels going into the employment market increase their chances of getting a job if they have relevant experience. Look through the advertisements in the newspapers. Many state 'experience preferred', 'must be experienced', or at the very least insist on some basic skills: computer literacy, a good telephone manner and the ability to work under pressure. The more competitive career areas, such as the media and professions, demand more experience than others – even from raw recruits.

Seeking experience

In a fast-moving world where international competition has arrived at every company's door and circumstances can change in an hour, organisations need people who will make a difference – *fast*. They want people who know about the workplace – preferably, their workplace. This is particularly true of small and medium sized businesses, which do not have the resources larger organisations have to spend on induction programmes. They need people who can hit the ground running within a very short time of their arrival at work.

Small and medium-sized firms are playing an increasingly important role in Britain's economy and offer exciting new ground for employment opportunities – but they also need people who can slide into work and get going from day one. Much effort is being made (through programmes such as STEP) to strengthen the relationship between small firms and universities, for example, so that companies understand how they might benefit from recruiting graduates. If you're at university or college, talk to your department and careers service to see if any such efforts are being made locally. You never know where your enquiry might lead.

Hitting the ground running

Experience means you're more likely to make an immediate contribution to the team effort. You're less of a hindrance and more of an asset. The veterinary nurse will be able to do far more to assist the vet – and the practice and therefore the business – if she has experience in dealing with animals and people, far more than someone who has no experience of handling either. Experience also means that you're more likely to familiar with all the information technology you'll inevitably come across in the workplace, and know what it's for and how to use it.

Training in basic skills

This doesn't mean that an employer doesn't have to train you at all in their ways. Every company will have its own way of:

- writing a business letter
- answering the phone
- using information technology.

Most organisations will, however, hope that your experience and basic knowledge of business life will enable you to know how to do

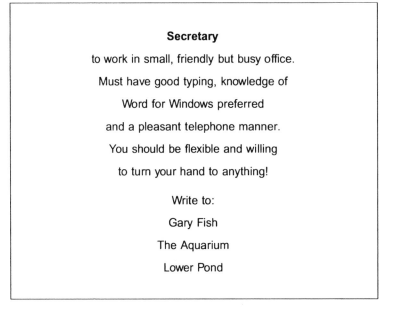

Fig. 1. A typical advertisement.

these things professionally. An understanding of their proper use can make a difference to a business.

Applying for a job

What does the advert in Figure 1 tell you about the job? Here's a rough translation:

- Small: Probably about ten to twenty people.

- Busy: Hectic pace, phones ringing, always under pressure. Friday hits you before you know it.

- Friendly: Social atmosphere, nice place to work.

- Good typing: Accurate, but not terribly worried about speed or the ad would specify one.

- Knowledge of W4W preferred: Your changes of getting an interview will be increased if you have this, but if they saw someone they really liked they might be prepared to train them.

- Flexible: Won't turn your nose up at making the tea, doing the more basic jobs, willing to switch from one job to another at a stroke.

- Write to: The employer has specified how you should contact him – by letter. So write.

The advert doesn't mention experience, but it does talk about **skills** – answering the telephone, typing and a knowledge of Word for Windows – and **personal qualities** – flexibility, the ability to work under pressure because the office is busy and not complaining when given the less demanding tasks. Enthusiasm, energy and a commitment to customer service, such as being pleasant on the phone and willing to serve and help others, are all vital ingredients to a successful career and to a growing business.

Increasing your employability
Imagine how your chances of getting this job would be increased if you:

- Knew how to use basic office equipment – the fax machine, photocopier, e-mail, voice mail, the Internet.

- Had practice in working in a similar environment so that you have basic knowledge of how an office works.

- Were able to relate your past experiences to situations that could arise in this office.

These skills could all be acquired on work experience and could increase your chances of getting that job.

Researching what the job will be about
This is crucial if you're going in for a profession which involves a long training, such as dentistry, veterinary surgery, medicine, teaching and law. You need to be aware of the less pleasant parts of the job as well as those that are enjoyable.

For example, any hotel manager will have to deal with guests who are a real pain, as well as those who are a joy to have to stay. Most guests will enjoy their stay but you always get one who seems to have been sent to make your life a misery. Could you deal with him effectively and professionally? Would you *want* to deal with an unhappy guest?

The moral of this example is that you need to know the downsides before you enter the business. Research gives you the power to make an informed choice about your career. Work experience is research.

Showing you're really interested in the job

Whatever you do, you need to have a passion for your work. If you don't, your chances of excelling decrease. Your performance will suffer. People these days are spending longer at work: the hours are no longer nine-to-five. Employers will look at how you've spent your spare time for proof of that passion, that spark that lights you up, turns you on and translates into action.

Passion leads to commitment, motivation, drive, a desire to learn and to do things in the right way, a willingness to work until the job is done, and to get up and do things without being asked. In short, it is more likely to ensure better service to the company's customers. If you can show that you know what you're letting yourself in for it makes you less of a risky recruit.

Choosing new members of a team

An employer is interviewing two students for a job in a small animation company. Ben comes in first.

Employer: So, Ben, when did you get some work experience in animation?

Ben: Well, the school organised that in the fourth year. We did three weeks. I went to a computer-aided design company. They couldn't place me at an animation company.

Employer: Did you do anything yourself to try to contact a company?

Ben: Umm, no.

Employer: And what about your spare time? What do you do?

Ben: Well, I play about on my computer a bit, play a bit of soccer with my mates, watch the telly. That sort of thing.

Employer: Do you do anything on your computer at home in the way of design?

Ben: Well, sometimes. We always do projects at school. Last term I designed a table for school children in primary classes. It held all their pens and stuff.

Ben leaves. The employer welcomes the next candidate, Andrew.

Employer: Well, Andrew, what work experience have you had in this line?

Andrew: We did three weeks' work experience at school – everyone does it. I spent time in an architect's office, most of which was spent on CAD. I enjoyed it, and it gave me a chance to see how CAD worked in a practical setting. But it wasn't really what I wanted, so I got my careers teacher to help me write to a company in London to see if I could spend a week with them in the holidays.

Employer: And what did you do there?

Andrew: Loads of stuff. I spent the week with a designer who was working on a series of cartoons for a magazine. I spent hours at night that week working on my computer trying to think of ideas myself. I've brought some of them with me, if you want to have a look.

Employer: What about in your spare time?

Andrew: I spend a lot of time on my computer – I'm either working on that or reading the latest magazines on PCs and so on. Plus I'm on the college swimming team, which takes up a lot of time.

In your view
- Who has done the most research into his career?
- Who has put in the most effort outside of school?
- Who shows the most commitment to anything?
- Who has gone the extra mile to pursue their career ambitions?
- Who shows the most enthusiasm for the work?
- Who would get the job?

This experience applies to people of any age, even if they haven't had a job before and even if the post offered promises that training will be given. Experience gained and research undertaken – particularly if you do it through choice in your own free time – shows that you are motivated to get up and achieve things. Employers like this sort of thing.

DEVELOPING SKILLS AND QUALITIES EMPLOYERS WANT

Some jobs need specific skills
In many areas of work – architecture, physiotherapy, engineering, nursing, for instance – employers need people with specific knowledge and skills acquired through rigorous training. Most of this knowledge will be gained through study on a full- or part-time basis, frequently at university or a college of higher or further education. Nonetheless, professionals in these areas will still need a wide range of skills in order to manage their day-to-day work and to meet the needs of their colleagues and clients.

All jobs need general skills
Every job needs different skills and qualities, but all jobs will require transferable skills. These include the ability to use and apply information technology, to communicate with others, to manage yourself and work with others. They are called **transferable skills**, because they transfer with you from one job to another. You can never lose them, only develop and improve them.

Work experience will help you:
- acquire new skills
- develop and improve existing ones
- prove to prospective employers that you can use your skills competently at work.

Developing a healthy attitude
Attitude makes a different and is important to employers. Which attitude is healthy and which is not? Jot down 'healthy' or 'unhealthy' at the end of each line.

- Never offering to help others who are under pressure:_____
- Staying late to complete a task without being asked: _____

- Complaining all the time: _____
- Taking solutions to your boss, not just the problem: _____
- Being an 'oh, I can't be bothered' sort: _____
- Spending fifteen minutes making a cup of tea, just to look busy: _____
- Looking to get things right the first time: _____
- Paying attention to detail: _____
- Seeking to improve your performance at work constantly: _____
- Not including 'oh, it'll do' in your vocabulary: _____
- Complaining loudly about your social life across the office: _____
- Leaving at exactly 5pm, even if you've got vital work to do: _____
- Regularly turning up late: _____

Employers gain an excellent idea of what your attitude is to work while you're with them on work experience. They know whether you are committed to getting things done, using your initiative, putting in a good hard day's work, wanting to do a good job, taking pride in the work you do and what the company stands for.

How healthy do you think your attitude is? Which of the above questions would apply to you? Can you provide examples of each 'healthy' answer, either through school work or outside class activities?

NETWORKING WITH PROSPECTIVE EMPLOYERS

Taking up opportunities to get some work experience will put you in touch with employers who recruit, maybe not immediately but at some time in the future. Don't forget that recruiting by placing an advert in a national or local paper can have advantages and disadvantages for the busy employer.

Looking at the pros of adverts
- A wide range of people will probably apply for the job – adverts cast a wide net.

- The advert reaches people that others methods of recruiting might not.

- Some of the people who apply may be useful in the future – a chance for the employer to build up a portfolio of possible recruits for the future.

Looking at the cons of adverts
- Hundreds of people may apply but the employer may still not get the person he wants.

- Advertising can be very expensive and waste a lot of time.

- Many small and medium sized companies don't have the resources to put into dealing with the large number of replies an advert could produce. They may prefer to recruit by word of mouth or taking on someone known to them.

Being known to potential employers
Recruiting people who are known to them is a welcome option for employers.

- They know how you might fit in to the company socially – a vital key to successful recruitment. Someone can have every qualification under the sun and be a disaster because socially they just don't fit and get along well with the rest of the team.

- They know what your attitude is like – whether you are naturally a 'get up and go' or a 'I can't be bothered' person and whether you're going to be a safe, reliable recruit for the organisation.

- You may be familiar with the company already and so be able to contribute more quickly; for example, you'll know about the organisation, what it does, who it deals with and who does what within it.

- They have a fair idea of your skills and competencies and how you can contribute to the company.

- It can save time and money – for the employer and new recruit!

- It reduces the risk element in recruiting.

GETTING A FOOT ON THE CAREER LADDER

Work experience can open the door to future employment. Below are some comments from people who have done work experience and been successful. They have promoted themselves and made the most of their experience.

- 'They've asked me back for the summer holidays.'
- 'They've offered me a job next year when I graduate!'
- 'They want to talk to me later on in my course.'
- 'They've asked me to come in and help out at Christmas.'
- 'They said I did really well, and offered me a reference if I apply for a job when I leave school/college/university.'
- 'They've asked me to their Christmas party/office barbecue.'
- 'They said any time I was looking for a job, to get in touch with them!'

Thinking about careers and work

Assessing positive outcomes
- 'I loved my placement – now I know I really want to be a dental nurse.'
- 'It was interesting to see how numeracy was used in work!'
- 'They gave me lots of helpful advice about choosing my courses for university.'
- 'It boosted my confidence.'
- 'I know now I want to work for a small/large company.'
- 'It was nice to be treated as an adult, for once – not like at school.'
- 'They told me how you train to become an RSPCA inspector.'
- 'I coped with it! My confidence has leapt bounds.'

Whatever your reasons for doing work experience and whatever your age, there are tremendous advantages to be had. Some of these may not be as obvious as they first appear:

Assessing less obvious outcomes

- 'Now I know that working in a large organisation is not for me.'

- 'I almost applied for law. Work experience showed me it wasn't for me.'

LOOKING AT LIFE AS EXPERIENCE

Gaining experience through paid work

This includes full- or part-time jobs, holiday work, Saturday jobs and seasonal work.

Doing unpaid work with a course in education

This covers unpaid experience which comes with a course in education – for example, a two-week placement in a garage for a motor vehicle engineering student.

Gaining experience through work via school, college or university

This kind of work experience may last for one day, a week, two weeks, three weeks or longer. You may be given the choice of where you do your work experience from a list of companies, or asked to find your own placement or told where you're going. If work experience is compulsory you'll always find some people who don't want to do it, while others look forward to going out on placement. A positive attitude is vital to a successful placement.

Thinking about yourself and your experience of life

You can build your experience in all sorts of ways through a wide variety of activities. Often, it doesn't really matter how you acquired that experience. What is more important is the way in which you make use of it afterwards, whether in applying for a job or course, or handling a certain similar situation. Too often, applicants tell an employer, 'Well, I haven't done much, really...'. Don't fall into this trap. Your experience counts. Use it to your advantage.

Which of the following have you done?

	Yes	No
Voluntary work	☐	☐
Casual jobs	☐	☐
Part-time jobs	☐	☐

Held positions of responsibility	☐	☐
Participated in team activities	☐	☐
Done a task to help somebody else out		
e.g. babysitting, taken care of next door's pet	☐	☐
Raised a family and run a home	☐	☐
Worked abroad	☐	☐

In Chapter 6 we'll analyse these activities for the skills you've acquired through them.

> **Think positively: the more you know about what you want to get out of work experience, the more valuable it will be – and the more you will gain from it. Take the opportunity and you may end up with a high profile within the firm, leading to a paid job!**

QUESTIONS AND ANSWERS

Can I organise my own work experience outside of any course requirements?

Yes, you can. The placement can be as long or as short as you like – organised by you independently of your school, college or university. Most employers will be delighted that you're organising it yourself: it shows motivation and commitment – qualities they appreciate.

I haven't really got any experience, but I have got involved in lots of activities in my spare time. I'm the treasurer for our school drama group and I'm involved in the school bank which has been set up. Does this count as experience?

The good news is that yes, it does. Any activity you do outside of a formal education or work setting will interest an employer because it means that you have got up and done something, completely off your own bat. Plus, taking the example of the student above, being treasurer involves developing skills like record-keeping, liaising with banks to set up an account, advising the leader of the group's financial situation, possibly going out to raise some more money. There are lots of skills that you can acquire through spare time activities, but you need to keep track of what you're learning.

Surely the experience organised by school is sufficient? A couple of weeks is a long time. Isn't anything else really cheap labour?

There are some employers who are going to make the most of having you around; you may find yourself working ludicrously long hours for no pay. An option is to ask for new responsibilities which will develop your skills further. If this idea is not well received, you may need to call it a day. A key skill to a successful career at work is knowing when it's time to move on. And remember – the more planning you do for what you want out of a placement, the more satisfying it is likely to be. Ultimately, you're investing time and effort into your career planning, which is never wasted. Work experience organised by your school, college or university *isn't* enough on its own any more. It's your future. Invest in it.

SUMMARY

- Experience gives you a strategic advantage.

- You have referees you can draw on for references.

- You have an opportunity to develop basic skills which employers need.

- You can experience a career area and decide for yourself whether or not it's for you.

- You can prove your interest and commitment in a career area, especially if you have done work experience voluntarily.

- Work experience puts you right where the action is – in the heart of an organisation.

CASE STUDIES

John wants to decide about his future career

John is studying for his GCSEs. He doesn't have a clue what he wants to do, but his parents and the school want him to stay for A-levels and John isn't bothered either way. At least, he thinks, it will put the decision-making process off and keep everyone quiet. After the exams are over the school organises work experience for three weeks. John discovers that he is going to work in a shop. 'I don't want to do retailing,' he thinks, but many of his friends weren't that inspired by their placements either. 'Make the most of it,' John's mother tells him. 'After all, you may end up with a summer job,' she jokes.

Susan wants to be a vet

Susan is desperate to be a vet, but for her school work experience, she is placed in a medical practice, helping the office staff there. She learns about record-keeping, how information technology can be applied at work and about how to deal with the public. She admires the way the receptionists handle the patients, who can be aggressive and demanding. 'Well,' one receptionist tells her one day while they are discussing Susan's career plans, 'it's the same in a vet's surgery – you need these skills if you're going into practice. People get very uptight when they take pets in to see the vet.' Susan has developed some transferable skills and gained insight into how a business is organised at the grass roots level, something which will be invaluable if she has her own practice later.

Mary returns to the workplace

Mary's children have grown up and she wants to return to work, partly because she wants to have some more money for herself, but also because she wants to do something different. She is worried about coping with all the information technology and returning to work after so long.

Mary goes to her local Adult Education centre and sees a careers counsellor. She admits the thought of returning to work terrifies her, but the counsellor explains that the course Mary is interested in contains work experience with companies who welcome mature students. Encouraged, Mary signs up for an office management course.

2

Identifying Your Needs

ASSESSING YOUR MOTIVATION

There are many advantages to doing work experience. Even if you
have been bored at work, at least you know what it's like to do
routine tasks. You'll have a better idea of what motivates people
doing the more mundane work, what their concerns are and how to
handle them – plus you'll appreciate how important their
contribution is to a company. You can learn from every situation
and all your colleagues at work – if you want to.

Planning ahead

Work experience will help you to plan your career. It will give you a
focus and put you in an empowering position, because you'll be
learning. Information you gather about yourself, the workplace and
what it takes to be at best successful, or at least survive, is power.
Work experience will shift your confidence up several gears and put
you in the driving seat, so that you have more control of your career.

Organising your own work experience
This may sound daunting, but if you write an action plan it will
make your task easier. Figure 2 gives you an idea of what's involved.

Working out what you want

Work experience is about learning.

> **The more you take control of your own learning programme,
> the more likely you are to get what you want out of it.**

If you drift into an office or company not knowing what you want to
get from your time there, you're likely to feel lost, useless, less
confident about asking for help and even defensive, bored, fed up
and angry. You'd be wasting your time and the company's. And

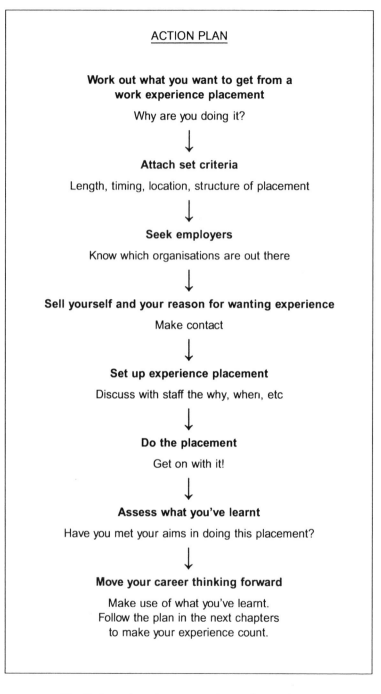

ACTION PLAN

**Work out what you want to get from a
work experience placement**

Why are you doing it?

↓

Attach set criteria

Length, timing, location, structure of placement

↓

Seek employers

Know which organisations are out there

↓

Sell yourself and your reason for wanting experience

Make contact

↓

Set up experience placement

Discuss with staff the why, when, etc

↓

Do the placement

Get on with it!

↓

Assess what you've learnt

Have you met your aims in doing this placement?

↓

Move your career thinking forward

Make use of what you've learnt.
Follow the plan in the next chapters
to make your experience count.

Fig. 2. An action plan to organise work experience.

you'd probably start making mistakes. Errors at work, unlike many of those you make at school or college, cost money.

Showing how you planned your career
Employers often ask you to explain how you came to choose the career you have. For example, they may ask you in interview why you chose the course you did. 'How did you decide to specialise in marketing, as opposed to doing a straight business studies course?' They like to see how you have managed your career planning and decided what your career goals are.

INVESTIGATING A CAREER AND PROVING YOUR INTEREST

Why investigate a career at all? Checking that it's the right one for you is vital if you are going in for a career or profession which involves a long and expensive training prior to qualifying and finding work.

It is also important to be able to show an employer you've done your research. A major complaint of employers at interview is that many people haven't done much research into:

1. The job they are applying for.
2. The industry they want to work in.

'People turn up for interview knowing literally nothing about this industry. You wonder why they haven't done any research – and whether they are really that interested in it and committed to it.'

Personnel manager, high street bank

Research will increase your changes of success and mean that you are more likely to find the right niche.

Going on a fact-finding mission
You can learn a lot by talking to people in the world of work. Most of them are keen to help and will happily tell you about their job. It does, after all, occupy a major part of their lives. Some may be reluctant to give you any indication of their salary; this is very personal information so it may be better to check books such as

Occupations (see Further Reading), look at adverts or contact the appropriate professional body for details.

Questions you should be asking

The answers to some of these questions may change over time, so always get up-to-date information from the right professional body. In the meantime, here are some questions you could start asking people at work.

- How long did they take to qualify?
- What sort of qualifications are needed to enter training, eg A-Levels/GNVQs, GCSEs? A degree? None at all?
- What sort of personal qualities do you need for the work?
- Who are your customers?
- What's the best thing about being a ... ?
- What's the worst thing about being a ... ?
- What hours are you expected to work?
- What does the job/career involve doing in any one working day?
- Are there any restrictions which make it difficult for individuals to get into that field, eg colour vision, height, age?
- What scope is there for setting up your own business?
- How is the work stressful?
- How can you best prepare for this line of work: eg work experience, evidence of interest needed by professionals?
- What other careers are related to this line of work?
- What is happening in the field locally, nationally, internationally?
- What else could you do after training for this line of work?
- Is it a growth industry/career area?
- What other factors affect its growth?
- How much are you likely to earn?

Which careers would you like to check out?
Make notes below of your areas of career interest:

My main area of career interest is: ....

Related careers are: 1. ....

2. ....

3. ....

Now you can look for employers and organisations in this line of work to approach for work experience. The careers book *Occupations* gives information about different careers and provides a useful cross reference from one career to another, so that you can make sure you're not missing something!

Proving your commitment to a career

If you are thinking of a career which involves lengthy training for a specific job, such as dentistry, veterinary science, medicine or nursing, get as much experience as you can in as wide a variety of settings as possible. Get your hands dirty by doing jobs lower down the scale; show that you can work well with a wide variety of people and that you're not afraid to muck in and get involved. Turning your nose up at the lower level jobs will make an employer question your commitment and dedication. Eventually you'll have a chance to observe or participate in the more responsible tasks after you've proved yourself. Remember too that professionals will want to have a good look at you before asking you back for more! Be pleasant, polite, cheerful and work hard and you'll open more doors.

Keeping a record of your experiences

Record all your visits to firms and participation in open days of any sort, indeed anything you've done which is related to your intended career. Make sure that your referees know about them so that they can mention them on any references. Ask your employers for a reference to go to your referee and ask the referee to quote from the reference. Support from a professional in the field provides evidence of your interest and commitment and gives you something to talk about with the interviewer.

Broadening your horizons

Try to get a wide range of experience, if you can. In the medical field, for example, this might mean caring for elderly people in a residential or nursing home during your summer vacation, or helping at a childcare centre for two weeks doing work experience. Both will improve your ability to relate to a wide variety of people – essential in any career involving patients. If you were considering entering a profession such as accountancy, you might want to try to gain experience in the public and private sectors, both of which offer accountancy training. Being able to compare and contrast your experiences in any part of your application shows an employer that you really have done your research and, equally importantly, it will point you in the right direction.

Confirming that your intended career is right for you
This is important, particularly if you're going into a profession such as teaching, anything clinical or very knowledge-based. You can always change career later on – many engineers go on into management, doctors may move into medical sales, vets into writing! – but because areas like these involve long training you must confirm that they are right for you. Work experience will help.

Supplying evidence to admissions tutors
Teaching, training and developing people costs time and money. One of the things admissions tutors will immediately look for, therefore, is evidence that you've really made an effort to go out and get lots of experience in a very wide area around the career.

LEARNING ABOUT THE WORKPLACE

Be happy at work! You're going to spend a lot of time there so it's important to think about the sort of organisation you want to be with. Life has a much better quality if you can look forward to going in to work.

Different organisations suit different people
Work experience gives you a good insight into organisations and their cultures. It will allow you to get a feeling for whether you want to be in a large or small company, for example; the two are very different. Your views may of course change as you get older.

Take an example: uniforms. Would you want to work in a profession or career that demands a uniform, such as nursing, cabin crew or the forces? Some organisations may also ask staff to wear uniforms, others won't. There are pros and cons of wearing a uniform to work.

Advantages of wearing a uniform
- You don't have to think about what you're going to wear each day.

- It may be bought for you by the company, thus saving you money.

- It may even be cleaned at the employer's expense, or you may get an allowance.

- It can encourage company loyalty.

- It's easier for the customer to identify staff.

Disadvantages of wearing a uniform
- You may tire of wearing the same thing.

- You may not like it.

- You may prefer to be able to choose what you wear to work.

   'When I went to college, I was really pleased because I could choose what I wanted to wear every day instead of sticking to a uniform. But now that I'm working, I'm really pleased to be wearing a uniform. I don't have the hassle in the mornings of deciding what I'm going to wear to work.'

Lee, retail organisation

Considering company culture is something that you can be thinking about while you are in the workplace. Every organisation will have its own 'feel'; you need to find one which you are comfortable with.

Learning about behaviour in the workplace
Work experience in any situation will teach you how to behave at work. Organisations will clearly vary in terms of formality, but they will expect customer service to be of the highest quality. You'll learn how to adapt your behaviour, dress, language and tone accordingly.

Getting experience through a part-time job
You may have worked already, perhaps through part-time jobs after school, during the school holidays or on a Saturday, in a previous

---

WEEK AT CLEARVIEW INDUSTRIES STARTING 25 JULY

Goal

To learn about the departments in an organisation.

- What do they do?
- How do they differ?
- What do they contribute to the company as a whole?
- Would any of them hold interest for me?

Action

Monday	Personnel Department
Tuesday	Information Technology Team
Wednesday	Sales and Marketing
Thursday	Production Department
Friday	Finance Department

Follow up

- Produce a two-page report for organisation on the way they all worked together.

- Discuss experience with careers officer in interview.

- Look at college courses which relate to those areas that interested me.

- Go back for more experience with that department for a week.

Fig. 3. Planning a work shadowing placement.

career, or through work experience on a course or at school. This will have offered you the chance to:

- earn some money

- acquire a reference from your employer

- meet an employer who was probably interested in your career and could point you in the direction of people who may be able to help

- gain a grounding in qualities that are needed at work, such as standards of behaviour and coping with the working day.

If you are an active learner, you can easily pick up a great deal of knowledge about what the workplace is all about and what it takes to be successful, as an individual and an organisation.

Gaining insight into the world of work

There are a number of ways you can learn about the world of work:

• spend time in one department or with one person

• spend a day with different parts of one business, or at least different people within it.

Gemma has chosen to spend time in different parts of a business at Clearview Industries, as her programme in Figure 3 shows. By spending time with staff in each section, Gemma will be able to understand:

– what that section does: its role and responsibility within the overall organisation

– how it is important to the company's work

– how it contributes to the company's goals

– how all the sections link together and support each other

– the people who work in that section and how they work together

– the different careers available in each one and the skills, qualities and qualifications needed to succeed in them

– whether they would be of interest to her

– how things happening throughout the world can affect the world of work

– what it takes to be competitive and survive – or excel. (One day, she may want to run her own business.)

Gemma comes up with new career thoughts

Gemma came away from Clearview Industries with a new career idea:

'Before going to Clearview I hadn't thought of a career in production engineering. Now I'm really interested; I've been back for more experience there and I think I've found my future career! I'm going to look for a course which includes production engineering and management studies, so that I can keep my options open.'

Gemma, sixth form student

Learning what it's like to be at work
If your reaction is: 'I've no idea what I want to do', take action!

- Talk to your careers adviser. Before you meet, write down the things you have an interest in and are good at, so that you can look at suitable careers together.

- Participate in computer-aided guidance tests. Schools, colleges and universities should all have access to these. They will point you in the direction of possible careers that might interest you.

- Don't decide on a career just because you like the sound of it and it will save you the bother of career planning any more.

Following your discussions with your careers adviser, target three or four areas of employment (not very specific careers) which you think might appeal. Use those to gain work experience in and start your research.

GETTING INSIGHT INTO LIFE AT THE TOP

Some work shadowing schemes offer you the chance to see what life is really like at the top of a company. You can shadow a manager or managing director for a week and see what makes a leader.

Thinking about what makes a leader
If you were to think of business leaders now, who would you name? Think of three or four. What is it about those people that have made them stand out to you? How have they made their mark in your mind? Take one of them and jot down four things that have made them stand out for you.

1. ....
2. ....
3. ....
4. ....

Aiming to be a leader or manager

If you want to find out about life at the top or in management, there are courses you can attend to find out more. For example, university students have access to Insight into Management Courses, run by the Careers Research and Advisory Centre; at school you have the opportunity to try your hand at running a company yourself through schemes such as Young Enterprise or work shadowing programmes. They all provide an excellent chance for you to try your hand at life at the top, perhaps by forming your own company, as in Young Enterprise, or by actually watching someone who is at the top of a company and spending time with them.

Could you lead and manage others? Try your hand and find out! You could be surprised and love it. If you make mistakes, learn from them.

MEETING COURSE REQUIREMENTS

Increasing numbers of courses involve work experience on an optional or compulsory basis. Many **GNVQ**, **HND** and **degree** programmes, for example, offer a placement as part of the course. People with relevant experience tend to find it easier to get jobs – many of them are offered jobs by the employer they've done the experience with. Students taking **NVQ**, **HNC** and part-time **degree** programmes will usually be in work anyway, attending college one day a week or in the evenings.

Finding information about requirements

If you're going out on work experience as part of your course, there are some things you will need to find out about, preferably before you start the course.

The most crucial aspect will be whether you are expected to find your own placement or if the college finds it for you. If the former, the earlier you start your search for an employer who will take you on, the better because:

- You're more likely to find a firm which really appeals to you.

- You will be better prepared, because you can take the chance to visit and get involved with the firm prior to your placement.

- You'll have more choice – you're beating everyone else to it!

Questions you'll need to ask
- Will you be assessed? If so, how?

- What will the work consist of – a project, day-to-day routine tasks, or a combination of both?

- Will you have the chance to visit your placement before it starts (you should do)?

- Will your course tutors visit you during your placement?

- Are you assigned a supervisor while you're at the company?

- Who should you turn to if things aren't going right?

- How will the work experience contribute to your course?

- Have any past students who have done work experience with the company got jobs there?

Being an ambassador
If you're doing work experience as part of a course, you are actually carrying a tremendous responsibility. When you go out for your work experience you're acting as an ambassador.

Represent yourself
Work experience provides an excellent chance for you to show an employer what you can do. Many employers recruit future workers through work experience placements. It gives them a chance to see how you fit in.

Be an ambassador for your course
Employers learn a lot about the calibre of a course by taking people on for work experience. It enables them to see what you, as a typical student, are learning and how well you can apply the theory you've

learnt in class to a practical setting. If they are impressed with you, they are more likely to offer a much needed place for work experience the following year.

Fly the flag for your institution
The employer may not know a lot about your institution, but will learn a lot about it as a teaching establishment from your performance and attitude. They will give feedback to your college or school, not just on your performance, but also on how well the course has prepared you for the workplace.

QUESTIONS AND ANSWERS

I don't want to go on work experience. We have to do it as part of our GNVQ course but I hate the thought. Help!

Try to assess why you're dreading work experience. Talk through the possible reasons with someone you trust. Visit the company before you start if you're nervous, it will make walking in on the first day a little more relaxing. Try to be open-minded; you never know, you may actually enjoy it!

What if they offer me a job, starting straight after my placement and I'm on a full-time course?

Lucky you! This does happen when students have done particularly well and an employer wants to keep them on. You'll need to weigh up the advantages and disadvantages of remaining in full-time education. One possibility could be to see whether it's possible for you to study on a part-time basis for the same qualification. The employer may even be willing to sponsor you. Talk it through with the employer and your college careers officers before making a decision.

I'm dreading the unexpected. How will I cope?

As you meet different people and new situations your confidence will develop and you'll feel able to handle anything that life throws at you. No one will give you anything to do they don't think you're capable of; if they thought you should be able to do the job when you arrived, you'd be in the position yourself!

DEVELOPING YOUR SKILLS AND PERSONAL QUALITIES

Employers need to recruit people who have:

- communication skills, both oral and written
- numerical skills
- information technology skills
- the ability to learn and to plan their career development.

You'll have a chance to find out how adept you are at these skills in the workplace but there are some others which you will also have a chance to practise.

Looking at transferable skills

The chart below lists some transferable skills required by employers (although some employers will place more emphasis on one skill than another).

1. Assess your skills as they are at present by ticking the column which applies to you now. Provide an example of how you have used each skill.

2. Show your rankings to someone you trust – a tutor, teacher, friend or someone who works. Would they agree with your rankings? Discuss them together.

3. Identify your strongest skills and those you enjoy using most, and then your weakest ones.

4. Seek ways to develop and assess your strengths and weaknesses on your work experience placement.

Assessment after your placement
Chapter 8 shows this chart again, so that you can make another ranking after your placement. If the placement has been effective you should be able to move your skills up a notch, and the skills you enjoy using the most and are best at will probably remain the same. This can give you confidence to plan your career using those skills.

Developing your personal skills

There are many ways to develop these. Here are some examples:

Skills set	Very good	Quite good	Average	Not good	Poor
Anticipating and adapting to change					
Working as a team					
Leading others					
Planning and organisation					
Establishing priorities					
Allocating resources					
Setting goals					
Meeting targets					
Analysing information					
Making decisions					
Solving problems					
Customer service					
Business awareness					
Negotiating					
Presenting material					

Try your hand at leading others
These may include:

- Young Enterprise
- Duke of Edinburgh Award Scheme
- president of a group
- chair of a committee
- leading a group activity
- running a local campaign
- leading a project.

Test your motivation and drive
Again, you can use lots of areas outside work to prove you have these qualities:

- planning an event and seeing it through from start to finish

- finishing things you started, even though it got tough along the way.

A major complaint of some employers is that younger recruits give up too easily when things get tough. Can you challenge this view with an example of how you've kept going to the finish in your own life?

Show you're willing and able to learn
An open-minded approach to learning, and an eager mind to build up knowledge independently of any direction from anyone else, will stand you in good stead. Do you regularly update yourself on your areas of interest by reading around them?

Examine your ability to get on with a wide range of people
If you're given a project to do with others, or if you are on a new committee, are you able to settle down and get to work quickly with them? Can you listen to what they have to say, and persuade them to change their views or compromise your view for the sake of the group?

Look at your ability to challenge, to question, to debate
Within the past three months have you:

- challenged a friend about an action they were taking that you thought was wrong?

- debated an issue and won someone round to your point of view?

Increase your confidence
Life always delivers the unexpected and work experience will teach you how to handle that. Your confidence will leap bounds as you deal with:

- customers suddenly demanding work by a tight deadline

- priorities which are changed because of a phone call

- meetings that have to be rearranged

- social arrangements which have to be altered because work demands it

- projects which have to be completed within a tight deadline.

Assessing what you want to achieve
You can see that there are a number of different reasons for doing work experience. If you have come up with another, add it.

Ranking your reasons
Below, rank your reasons for seeking work experience from one to six in order of importance to you. This exercise will help you focus on:

- what you want to achieve most from work experience

- the sort of organisation you will need to target for help

- the people you will want to be with during the experience.

I want to do work experience to:

1. Investigate a career and prove my interest in it ....

2. Consider company culture ....

3. Learn about the workplace ....

4. Get insight into life at the top ....

5. Meet course requirements ....

6. Develop my skills and personal qualities ....

Added bonuses

Adding to your CV

By the end of your experience placement you should also be able to expand your CV with a new range of skills and experiences, which you can highlight to a prospective employer.

Getting paid

Do you want to get paid for your experience? Or at least receive room, food and pocket money plus travel costs? Many programmes offer you the chance to gain experience through being in the workplace or doing voluntary work. For some you'll get room, board and pocket money; for others, you'll get some money and travel costs. They all vary, so have a good hunt around until you find one that suits your needs. Temping is also an ideal way to earn money while gaining experience in the workplace.

SUMMARY

- Have clear idea of what you want to achieve on work experience – you'll be a far more active learner.

- Work experience is a useful way to learn about yourself and what you want in life.

- If you don't have any career plans, get advice sooner rather than later.

- Don't be afraid to ask for advice and help – most people at work are keen to give it.

CASE STUDIES

John doesn't think about his motivation

John has to investigate careers in retail while on work experience and report his findings to his classmates in a presentation. When he attends the interview prior to his placement, the interviewer asks him what he wants to get out of his experience. John tells her about the project.

'I wasn't asking what the school wants you to do,' the interviewer says. 'What do *you* want to get from it? How can we help *you*?' John is ashamed to admit that he doesn't know. His supervisor asks him to think carefully whether he really wants to spend his placement with them. John feels very embarrassed – he realises that the employer *does* want to help him.

Susan proves her point

Susan finds out as much information as she can from the professional body for veterinary surgeons and gets experience at riding schools, pet shops and a kennel before approaching a local vet to ask for a week's work placement. She knows she has to prove her interest in working with animals to the vet, no matter how dirty or tiring the work, if he is to take her on.

Mary identifies her key task

Mary has signed up for an office management course and, having spent one-and-a-half terms in the classroom, she wants to see how her IT skills are in the workplace. At the same time her course demands that she spends two weeks in an office environment. Mary is placed in the IT department of an accountancy practice which is in the middle of training staff to use the newly installed computer system. To prove her commitment to helping the firm, she finds out what she can about it before she starts. Her new employers are impressed by her research.

3

Planning the Details

In planning your work experience you need to consider:

- How long you want it to be.
- When do you want to do it?
- Where do you want to do it: home or away?
- Do you want to watch someone or do things?
- Do you want to be with one person or several?
- Is there an application deadline? (If relevant.)

CONSIDERING LENGTH OF PLACEMENT

The length of a placement will depend on factors such as:

- Whether you are doing it as part of a course; there could be a specified amount of time you must spend on work experience.

- Whether it has been organised by your school for a set period of time.

- Whether you are doing it off your own bat.

- How long the company can offer you.

A placement could be for:

- one academic year
- one day, morning or afternoon a week for a term
- a block two or three-week placement
- a week
- the summer holidays
- two or three years (with day release), for example in an Apprenticeship
- other.

Choosing the appropriate length

Usually, the longer the placement the more likely you are to get something out of it, but that depends on the reason for your going on work experience. You could also find yourself with time restraints, such as if you are seeking to change career and are already working. Various lengths of placement have their different uses.

Afternoon
- Will give you a snapshot picture; you'd have to be able to pick up things quickly.

- Unlikely to be asked to do anything terribly concrete in an afternoon.

- Unrealistic picture – the office could be unusually quiet/busy.

- Could be organised as a school/college/university visit as a group.

But

- You still make contacts.

- It could lead to further placements.

- It's enough to get information about training, qualifying and advice.

- It's enough to get an insight into what a company looks like from the inside.

Three weeks
- A good length of time in which to develop skills.

- Better knowledge of what goes on over a number of weeks.

- A chance to prove yourself and to make contacts.

- Would enable you to do a small project.

- In summer you could do three weeks back-to-back, each with different companies.

But

- Can take out quite a chunk of, say, the holidays – therefore it is also a good signal of your motivation.

Six months/year

- Proof of motivation, dedication and commitment.

- Excellent chance to develop strong work-related skills and knowledge and to put classroom theory into practice.

- Lengthy commitment, but very useful on your CV.

- Chance to gain understanding of how businesses change over a period of time.

But

- It could be tough financially, although the company may well pay you. If this is part of your higher education course, find out how your university or college will assess you, how often they will visit you and how they will help you.

WORKING OUT WHEN TO DO IT

Figure 4 illustrates the wide range of opportunities available for you to get work experience under your belt:

Fig. 4. Finding time for work experience.

Choosing the right time

If you're setting up the placement on your own, you can decide when is best for you. Holidays vary in their effectiveness:

Christmas
- Many people try to take time off to be with family and friends or make the most of their holiday allowance; you may find you can easily fill in.

- On the other hand many organisations are quieter over Christmas and New Year so you may not get the real picture.

Easter
- Could interfere with exam revision timetable.

- Could also be a useful time to meet with a company to set something up for the summer.

Summer
- A useful period when many people are away and employers may need someone to help out.

- A good length: you can get to know the firm pretty well and they get to know you; you are more likely to be able to do things.

- Could interfere with travel plans you may have.

More and more businesses function 24-hours a day

If you think it's going to be difficult to get work experience during the traditional 9-5 day, fear not. All sorts of organisations now open for longer during the week and at weekends because their customers and a global market demand it. It's easier to get experience outside of 'normal' hours than it used to be.

A point on age

By law you cannot take part in any hands-on activities until your last year of compulsory schooling (ie, before Easter in Year 10). Watch, listen and learn instead.

DECIDING HOW FAR TO TRAVEL

You have a number of options:

- Stay at home, where you probably know more people so it may be easier to set up a placement.

- Stay in your university town, again you probably have more contacts.

- Go to another part of the country where you know accommodation won't be a problem, perhaps staying with friends of the family or relatives.

- Go abroad.

- Join a volunteer work (abroad) programme where accommodation is provided.

Where you go may depend on what you want to achieve and how long you want to take doing it. Getting a placement abroad means you can:

- get experience
- enjoy life abroad and develop sensitivity to other cultures
- learn a language if you're in a non English-speaking country
- network overseas.

Finding somewhere to live away from home
You could check:

- adverts for job shares in local newspapers

- hostels in the area

- university/college accommodation which might be rented out in the vacations

- bed-and-breakfast.

If you go abroad, you could:

- organise some work experience before you go

- leave it to chance and see what happens; many people do pick up work casually, not necessarily in their chosen line but at least they're getting the cash.

Going abroad for work experience

Tom does Australia
Tom spent his university holidays in Australia doing casual work. Through his efforts, he can show he has these skills and qualities:

Jobs	Skill/quality
Drove a car from Melbourne	Clean driving licence Meets deadlines Reliable, trustworthy Adventurous
Worked in a bar	Sociable Can deal with wide range of people Can work under pressure Can handle money
Picked apples on a farm	Has done routine, boring work Used to hard work, probably in unpleasant working conditions Likely to be tough and resilient
Went to Australia to pick up work	Risk-taker Self-motivated
Got employment	Resourceful.

The employers Tom spoke to when he was job-hunting liked the fact that he had taken the risk and just gone, playing his situation by ear. They appreciated his resourcefulness in making contacts for work and keeping to a low budget – something he would have to get used to in the future!

Planning for work abroad

- Plan well in advance – some work experience programmes have lengthy application deadlines.

- Check you have good health insurance coverage.

- Ensure you've got a valid passport and a visa to work, if you need one.

- Make sure you've got enough money to get home again.

- Get a contract outlining the work you'll be doing, and when and how you'll get paid.

- Find out whether your new employer will contribute to your travel costs.

Contacting international organisations

If you want to get work experience abroad, you could approach organisations with international connections and ask for help:

- International community service organisations, such as local Rotary or Lions Clubs who actively seek to encourage international understanding.

- Exchange programmes run by these organisations, as well as your school which could result in work experience through contacts made locally.

- Programmes such as BUNAC or Camp America, designed to give you that international experience.

- Companies advertising their career opportunities on the Internet.

- Businesses which have overseas branches.

Taking part in structured work experience programmes

There are now far more work experience programmes which have been set up specifically to give people – especially students – greater opportunities to work in other countries. This is particularly the case in the EU, where great strides have been made (and a lot of money poured into) developing work experience schemes. Your careers service and department will have all the information on what your particular institution has to offer. Find out sooner rather than later what all the options are.

COMPARING WATCHING AND DOING

What's the difference between work shadowing and work experience?

Work experience means learning how to do something by *doing* it. Work shadowing involves watching someone doing something. For example, you could watch what a company secretary does for a day to see what that job involves. Doing this will give you the chance to practise using specific skills and knowledge yourself.

Do you have to watch people all the time and go with them everywhere?

As a rule, yes. Sometimes, however, you'll find that the person has tasks to do – such as dictating a letter or reading a file – which means you are likely to get bored. In this case, you may find that you need to spend time with someone else. The idea of shadowing is that you do go to most places with them unless it's confidential.

Won't the person being shadowed find it irritating to have someone sitting beside them all day?

First, most people volunteer to be shadows. If they didn't want to be one, it wouldn't make sense for a company to offer them, because their lack of interest would show. Secondly, most shadows find that their observers offer a fresh approach, by questioning them about why and how they do things. Being watched makes them think, 'Why am I doing this?' But they will need to get used to you being there.

Getting practice in watching people at work
The next time you attend a class or a meeting, watch your teacher or chair. What skills have they had to use, prior to the class/meeting, during it and afterwards? What makes them a good leader?

Watching for safety reasons
In some cases you may need to watch rather than do because the equipment used needs very specific and careful handling and training. For safety reasons it would be dangerous for you to use it.

WORKING WITH ONE PERSON OR SEVERAL

You can learn a lot from watching others, particularly from the way in which they handle people. You need to think about whether you want to watch one person or several.

Advantages of spending time with one person

- You'll get an idea of what their typical day is like and what a specific role entails.

- You'll get to know them and, hopefully, develop a trusting relationship with them that enables you to ask the questions you want.
- They may offer to help later on in your career and even act as a mentor.

Disadvantages of spending time with one person

- It could be more interesting to contrast styles and ways of doing things if you're with several people.

- You may not like them, but persevere, it will take time for both of you to get to know each other.

- It can be less broadening in terms of your knowledge of jobs and careers.

Advantages of spending time with different people
- You'll gain a better understanding of the business as a whole.

- You'll see different styles in the way people handle situations and staff.

Disadvantages of spending time with different people
- You'll get a brief view of what each person does, as opposed to a thorough one.

- It's harder to see what the typical day entails as you're with people for, say, one day.

Considering other suggestions

The organisation you contact may have its own idea about how to handle work experience, or practicalities may force their hand.

You'll probably find that your time is divided between different people, because staff may be away on holiday/off sick/on a business trip. Listen, compromise and be flexible where necessary.

Have a Plan B – just in case
If you fail to get on that all-important work experience programme, why not consider other ways to get yourself noticed? Temping is one way to do this – you may work for several organisations as a temp and have a chance to compare your experiences in the different firms, and decide which one suited you best. It also provides you with an excellent chance to get your foot in the door and prove yourself to an employer – many companies recruit permanent staff through temping. The next chapter will give you some more information about going to recruitment agencies.

PLANNING YOUR EXPERIENCE

Now that you've read through this chapter, set out your logistics:

My goal on work experience is: ....

My preferred length of placement is:................................

I will be aiming for these dates (subject to the company's approval)

....

I want to be based: home/abroad

My activities will focus on: watching/doing/both

I will need help from: one person/a department/an organisation.

Now you're ready to look for employers who may be able to help you.

SUMMARY

- Think carefully about the logistics of doing a work placement.

- Be prepared to negotiate with an employer about when you do the placement.

- Remember that work experience can be gained abroad as well as at home.

- It pays to research your options early on as some programmes have lengthy deadlines.

- There are many work experience or work shadowing programmes available in Britain and further afield.

CASE STUDIES

John plans his time
John's school has told all the students that they have three weeks' work experience to do, plus a project to present. He realises that he also has a long working day, longer than the school one. 'Don't leave your project to the last minute,' the school advises, 'because you'll be tired by the end of your placement.' John looks at how he could use his time during the evenings and at weekends to prepare his project.

Susan works out timing and people
Susan wants to spend the October half-term on work experience, close to home to save on travel costs and to make it easier to get to the vet's surgery. She decides it would be useful to ask if she could spend time with the veterinary nurses, as well as the vet, to show that she recognises the role they play in the business. This impresses the practice – too many students forget the role nurses play.

Mary meets the firm's needs too
Many wants to see how the staff outside an IT department cope with the computer systems and what they are looking for in IT support. She asks if she can spend two or three days with these staff. The firm thinks this is a good idea and asks Mary to produce a written report on her findings.

4

Finding Employers to Help

Start finding an employer to help you by drawing up an action plan. Depending on the help and support available to you, your action plan will look something like the one below:

1. Note the sort of company you want to join, depending on your career interests.

2. Get names of companies who may be able to help you.

3. Find out more about them.

4. Make up a shortlist of employers to contact from your list.

MAKING USE OF YOUR NETWORK

Networking may be the key to success and is an important skill in the workplace. Your contacts may:

- know whether there might be a job in a particular place of work

- know who is recruiting generally

- know the names of personnel officers or managers in a particular organisation

- give you suggestions about firms which might be willing to help you

- be able to provide an introduction to a firm

- know of someone who could offer you a practice interview

- comment on your CV

- tell you about their career

- be able to offer you a job, eg in the holidays to get extra money, or a full-time post

- be able to give you work experience.

Who do you know who can help you?

Below is a list of people who may be able to help you get that work experience placement – and a job. Jot down anyone in each category who you know can assist you and you'll have made your network. Don't forget past schools and colleges – they will still be pleased to help you. Parents can also look to their offspring's school careers staff for help.

Careers teacher	Head teacher	Adult guidance tutor
Your parents	Members of governing body	Course tutor
Careers officer	Friends of the family	University tutors
School teachers	Friends' parents	Past employers
Parents' current employers	University careers services	School friends
Friends who work	Members of clubs you belong to	Local businesses you use
Organisations involved in school, college or university life	Past employers from Saturday/holiday jobs	Brothers/sisters
Relatives/friends living abroad	Word of mouth	People you meet through interests/hobbies
Employers giving talks in education	Employers met at careers conventions	College careers services
Employers listed in *Yellow Pages*	Local programmes set up by TECS/Careers Service	Year-out programmes
Local community organisations	Chance meetings	Professional organisations

Fig. 5. Forming your own network.

Essential rules of networking

1. Make sure you thank contacts who help you – you may need their help again.

2. Ask if there is anything you can do to help them.

3. Keep in touch with them and update them on your career.

4. Be polite and positive.

5. Don't be pushy if they can't help – you'll only get people's backs up.

Taking advantage of chance meetings

Make the most of the opportunities you have to meet people who are in full- or part-time work, whatever their age and occupation. They may have some sound advice for you, new names, ideas and suggestions. Ask them lots of open-ended questions, such as 'What do you do?', 'What does that involve?', 'Tell me about your line of work', and 'What would your advice be?' to get them going. Write to thank them for their help afterwards.

Keep track of names suggested to you
As you speak to them, make a list of those employers your contacts recommend who might be able to help. Put them in a folder or notebook, not on a scrap piece of paper that will get lost straightaway, and find out more about those organisations.

Using your network
Every one of these people will have their own network and many of them, in particular those within educational establishments, will know which employers are willing to offer work experience. All you have to do is ask.

Advantages of networking

- Each member of your network will have their own network of contacts, so you are spreading your knowledge even wider.

- It is good practice to learn how to network; it's a skill you'll need when you're in work.

- You'll learn a lot through the experience of making a direct approach through your network.

- You'll become confident through using your network.

- Many employers are impressed when people make a move off their own bat – it does take motivation and effort, which means you must be keen.

Disadvantages of networking
- People who think they know you best may try to persuade you to do something you don't really want to do so keep your focus.

- Those you are getting your advice from may not be up-to-date in their knowledge.

- You may need to explain the art of networking to others who don't understand what you're trying to ask of them.

FINDING EMPLOYERS TO CONTACT

Outside of your network, where can you find names of organisations which might be willing to help you? Here are some suggestions:

- The *Yellow Pages* phone book, available in all public libraries, will give you the names, addresses and phone numbers of organisations in your area.

- Local newspapers with recruitment pages will often include the names of the person in charge of recruitment. In a large company this is likely to be a personnel officer. In a smaller one it may be the boss. Jot down the name and address – and you've got a name to contact.

- Use information technology to help you. On the Internet many organisations have web sites with details about their career opportunities.

- Local recruitment agencies may specialise in a given sector of work, such as hospitality, childcare or IT; or they may be more generic, offering opportunities to work in a number of different areas. Walk down your local high street to get an idea of what sorts of companies are offering temporary work; check your local *Yellow Pages* too.

- Local recruitment agencies could help if you want to go temping. You may end up with a paid temporary job.

- Visit the library. Books such as *Kompass*, which lists all British companies, are especially useful if you're looking to do work experience outside of your home or university area, or you're looking for details of small and medium sized companies.

- Use trade magazines to look for prospective employers.

- Seek careers publications such as *Prospects* and *GET*, produced for prospective graduates. These publications advertise graduate vacancies for the current year. Why not see if they would be willing to give you some experience in the year before you graduate? You could end up solving their recruitment problems for them the following year.

- Check out the numerous organisations offering work experience for a period, perhaps abroad, such as GAP, CSV, STEP.

- Make use of your careers service early on to find out what's available. Many jobs go to the first applicants, so don't miss out. Visit the Prospects web site for lots of exciting details of work experience placements and programmes for university and college students, including the Work Experience Bank.

- Also try the career's service noticeboard, Job Shops, the Job Centre and local post office windows...

Dropping a letter in to an organisation
You could drop in to a company with a copy of your CV and a letter outlining your desire for work experience. First impressions count, so dress appropriately. The advantage of dropping in is that the person you're addressing your letter to may have a couple of minutes to spare and come out to meet you. Be ready to tell them why you're there in a few short sentences. Don't expect this, however, and don't complain if they are too busy to see you.

After you've dropped your letter in...
Call the person you addressed the letter to, two or three days later. They should have received the letter by then and had a chance to look through it. Find out whether they would be interested in meeting you to discuss your letter.

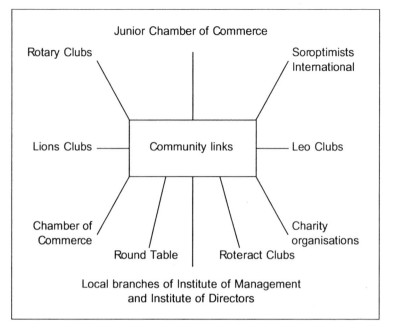

Fig. 6. Contacting community service organisations for help.

USING COMMUNITY CONTACTS

You could try writing to the presidents of community service or business organisations, as Figure 6 suggests. You don't have to ask for specific names, just say: 'I'm looking to get some work experience in... do you know of anyone or any organisation that might be helpful?'

These organisations want to help young people in one way or another, and you never know what sort of response you might get. Many are also international so you could end up with some useful links for going overseas.

Approaching community service organisations

Yellow Pages or the Citizens Advice Bureau should tell you how to make contact. Find out what each community service organisation does first, so that you can link what your needs are with their goals as an organisation.

You can offer to go and speak to them about your experience, and the sort of help you and your peers need in making career decisions. It will develop your presentation skills and your confidence.

DEVELOPING EXPERIENCE THROUGH VOLUNTARY WORK

Employers like to see voluntary work on a CV. It shows that you're committed, dedicated and motivated and that you don't just sit at home watching television. Employers like enquiring, creative minds which are enthusiastic and willing to go that extra mile for others. Voluntary work shows that you can deal with a wide range of people, that you've probably got qualities of resourcefulness, patience, care and putting someone above your own needs. It calls for initiative, creativity and planning. It will inevitably toughen you up and instil in you an ability to make the most of things.

Choosing from the variety on offer

There are so many voluntary schemes that finding one to suit your individual needs could prove harder than you think. Examples are:

- GAP Activity Projects
- Community Service Volunteers
- Kibbutz Reps.

Check Further Reading for books detailing such programmes.

The length varies as well, from one or two years to two or three weeks. Most will offer some or all of the following for your efforts:

- accommodation and food
- flights (where appropriate)
- pocket money.

Think about what you want to do. Do you want something that is related to your career thoughts, or not? Usually, people travelling and working just want to earn enough so that they can enjoy themselves and have a roof over their heads and enough to eat.

Plan well ahead
Many of these schemes have their application deadlines well in advance of the start of their programmes, because there is a lot to sort out. Get to your local library and local Careers Service early on and start looking through books such as *Work Your Way Around the World* – a mine of helpful information on programmes.

Targeting a few programmes

If you've picked up a book in your local library which lists lots of programmes and you don't know where to start, Figure 7 suggests a way to target schemes. Focusing usually gets results. If you follow the action plan you're more likely to find programmes that suit you. If you just pick up the book, and leaf through, it will take you much longer and you'll probably just get fed up.

Volunteer your services locally

You don't need to go abroad to build up useful skills through doing voluntary work. Many voluntary organisations will want help in your area; your local Citizens Advice Bureau or Students Union will give you some ideas of what is available. Fund raising, promoting, organising, caring, doing the accounts, teaching and selling are all examples of the sorts of skills you can develop through voluntary work. A positive approach and a willingness to help are the key qualities required to start with.

It is worth noting that voluntary work is often required to get a job in the charity sector – you'll see adverts saying, 'proven interest in conservation/heritage/buildings/animal welfare is expected'.

TAKING PART IN (SUMMER) WORK EXPERIENCE SCHEMES

Some organisations run (summer) schemes to give young people an introduction to their career and relevant experience. They can provide a useful way of introducing yourself to a company and showing what you can do, and you will probably get some sort of payment.

Finding out about (summer) schemes

Excellent sources of knowledge about company schemes will be your local careers service or university/college careers service. Start enquiring about them and writing to companies for information in the autumn term before you wish to go, so that you don't miss out and that you get ahead of the competition. This sort of experience is vital for areas like veterinary surgery, law, banking, accountancy, medicine, retail and the media.

Write to employers directly to ask whether they run such a programme, talk to your careers teacher, visit your local TEC or find out what the year above you did the previous year. If you're at university or college, make a bee-line for your careers service and ask for help.

Fig. 7. Finding the right sort of experience abroad.

Schemes for university students

Universities have lots of information about vacation opportunities; increasing numbers of companies offer work experience programmes and schemes, partly in an effort to assist in their recruitment drives the following year. The Shell Technology Enterprise Programme (STEP), for example, offers suitably qualified, well motivated students in their second or penultimate year the chance to work in small and medium sized companies for eight weeks during the summer holidays, working on their own project. Check under Useful Addresses for more details.

The benefits of (summer) work experience schemes

Summer schemes give you a chance to prove what you can do, to make contacts which could last you through your further and higher education course, provide evidence of interest to selectors – and give you some pocket money.

There are a variety of short programmes on offer:

- For students studying for degrees in any subject.
- For students studying for degrees in a specific area, such as engineering, computing and business studies.
- Sponsorship schemes, whereby the company gives you experience

during the summer and then sponsors you for the final year of your degree programme. These are mostly for students taking a relevant course.

- Short-term contracts, where you can at least explore what the workplace is like and get a reference.

- Open days or short stints during the Christmas holidays to give you insight into the company.

HAVING A YEAR OUT

Increasing numbers of employers are offering a year's work to students seeking to take a year out before they start at university. Some courses – such as agriculture – may insist on it so that you can be absolutely certain it's what you want to do.

Looking for work for a year
You could:

- Target companies with a letter outlining your skills and career interests. See if they could offer you a paid job for a year prior to your university course, or if they have a project they need someone to do.

- Enlist for temporary work with local recruitment companies which will give you greater insight into a wide range of businesses.

- Check with your careers tutor to see what past students did last year; you could well fill in where someone has left off.

- Talk to your local TEC – they may know of a business which could use your services – but you need to know very well what you have to offer.

Using recruitment agencies
Visit agencies (addresses in *Yellow Pages*) in a smart outfit with a copy of your CV and an idea of what sort of work you're best suited for. If you are finishing a term, it would be worth visiting the agency a few weeks beforehand so that you can get signed up before everyone else. Give them a call a couple of weeks before you are

ready to start, and then again every day to let them know that you want to work.

Joining a programme for one year or less
There are (paid) programmes such as the Year in Industry (see Useful Addresses), involving companies in areas like civil engineering, consultancy, computing, energy, IT, food and drink and transport.

There are advantages to joining such schemes. You can:

- develop skills such as teamwork, communication, organisation and planning

- learn more about life in industry and/or life in business

- use skills in information technology and numeracy

- mature and gain confidence

- save money while gaining experience

- perhaps get sponsorship

- change or develop your career plans

- network with prospective employers

- take a break from academic life and continue on to university feeling refreshed

- get ideas for possible projects to do as part of your university studies or for a post-graduate course.

TAKING THE NEXT STEP

You are now ready to contact employers. Follow these steps and you'll be ready to move on.

1. List any employers who might be able to help you.

2. Get as much information as you can on them through:
   - company brochures on products
   - news bulletins they produce
   - initial visit to look around
   - talking to someone who works there
   - careers literature

- newspapers
- the annual report
- spending a day there to see what you think.

3. Think about what they would be looking for in a work experience candidate:
   - what qualities would they want?
   - what skills would they want?

4. Now you're ready to move on to the next step: contacting them! Find out how government agencies may be able to help you, too. The next chapter will give you more information about this.

SUMMARY

- Make use of your network – you'll be surprised how extensive it is.

- Try to be creative when thinking of ways to search for employers.

- Your search will be more effective if you start planning early.

- Don't be afraid to ask for help if you're not having any luck finding an employer in your area.

- The more time you spend looking for the right employer, the more likely you are to find a firm which is right for you.

CASE STUDIES

John uses his network for advice

John's project involves talking to people at work to see what their advice would be to people choosing a career. He knows lots of people in employment and his mother suggests that he gives them a ring and talks to them prior to starting the placement. 'They might tell you how you can best deal with your first day,' she suggests.

'Get all your things ready the day before – you don't want to be hunting round in the morning for your clothes and lunch money,' his brother's friend tells him. His mate on the football team who works in a bank says, 'Don't be surprised if they give you easy stuff to do. They want to see how you handle that first and to build your confidence.' Another friend adds: 'Be yourself, relax, ask for help if you need it. And get rid of your earring.'

Susan seeks employers
Susan uses *Yellow Pages* to look for vets' practices. She also contacts all the people she has done some work experience with to see if they can suggest any more. One of them offers to contact his local vet for her. 'That's very kind of you,' Susan explains gratefully, 'but I think I should try to set this up myself. I would like to put you down as a referee on my CV if I can.' Susan's contact is delighted to help her and admires her wish to find a vet through her own efforts.

Mary does more work experience
Mary has done one stint working for a very supportive company. She now wants to go out and find one herself, to get practice in marketing and to see how she gets on in a more realistic situation. A friend of her husband suggests a new company which is just setting up in a business centre who, he knows, needs an office manager. Mary gets the details and puts her CV together. Could she offer her services?

5

Getting Help in Your Search

SEEKING ADVICE FROM CAREERS STAFF

Careers staff should have an excellent network of employers. This also applies to teachers or tutors who have charge of organising work experience for students. Even if they don't know of someone who can help you, they will probably be able to get in touch with someone who will know:

Student: 'I'd like to do work experience with a lion tamer.'
Careers teacher: 'I don't know any lion tamers... but I know a man who might. I'll have a word with him and get back to you.'

Letting careers staff know your needs

Careers teachers, tutors, counsellors and officers aren't mind-readers. They don't know what you want unless you tell them. Let them know what sort of help you need. If you haven't got a clue about your career plans, tell them and get some advice.

Work experience co-ordinators

Some schools and colleges in one area have a work experience placement officer whose job it is to place all those students going out on work experience. This ensures that the employers in the area are not besieged by requests from schools for work experience. Placement officers have tremendous contacts because it is their job to go out and drum up enthusiasm and help for work experience projects. You could make use of those and ask for help.

USING YOUR LOCAL TEC

Training and Enterprise Councils (TECs) are independent regional bodies created to assist local businesses in a global economy and to deliver more effective training and education programmes which meet the needs of local employers. People are the most important resource in any business and the TECs try to ensure that businesses will have access to a well-trained and qualified workforce. They network with government agencies, employer groups, the voluntary sector and anyone involved in training, education and employment – including individuals like you.

TECs offer more than training

TECs also try to develop the range of support services available to local businesses to help them grow and thrive in a competitive world. They initiate activities which are meant to foster growth, which will in turn lead to better job prospects for everyone in the community. Because they are in close contact with local businesses, they may know of companies who have projects or research that needs to be done. You could do this work as part of a course or for work experience (paid or unpaid).

Finding out about your local TEC

Check your telephone directory or local library – many TECs have literature in public libraries with details of the services they offer. Drop in and pay a visit, they will be delighted to help. Some of them may have introduced their own work experience programmes. In Scotland, TECs are known as **LECs** (Local Enterprise Councils).

You'll need to invest in training for yourself throughout your life now, so give them a call if you have any questions or want any advice about training and work experience programmes available in your area. Some TECs work with graduates to assist them find work and to enable employers to see how graduates might be of value to their organisations.

GETTING ON TO GOVERNMENT SCHEMES

As the government seeks to help people find their niche in the workplace, so the number of training programmes available to people of all ages has increased. Some, such as the Modern Apprenticeship programme, are geared specifically to people of a certain age, but most have a very individual approach and advisers will talk to you about what you want to achieve from the training programme and help you find you way to success. There are also initiatives such as the Work Experience Bank for students at university – check the Internet or visit your careers service for details.

Some schemes last until you find a job. Others, such as Apprenticeship programmes, may take two or three years, or longer, because they are properly structured programmes taking you through a qualification while you're at work. You may decide that, for you, they are viable alternatives to full-time education or remaining at home doing nothing. Let's have a look at what they can offer you.

Taking the opportunity
You'll probably have the chance to get:

- Work experience.
- A job.
- Training for a National Vocational Qualification, which proves that you can do the job and that you have the skills employers need.
- Training in broader transferable skills which will be of interest to another employer.
- Advice on your career development.
- Help with job applications.
- Various types of financial support, ranging from help with travel expenses to extra benefit and childcare support; these do vary from scheme to scheme.

In the case of the Modern Apprenticeship scheme, you'll get a training allowance or be paid a wage or salary by an employer.

Getting more information
Your local careers officer or TEC will be able to provide this. You may find that some schemes offer limited places, so apply early.

'Aren't they just cheap labour?'
Government schemes have often had dubious reputations, partly because they are run by the State. But now private training firms are also offering work placements and many schemes are employer-led, so this should increase their effectiveness. Of course, a lot depends on the attitude of those on the scheme, and their ability – and motivation – to take responsibility for their own learning and development.

What apprentices say about the advantages
- 'I'm sure it will lead to better job opportunities.'

- 'I'm getting experience while training – a brilliant combination.'

- 'I'm learning lots of new skills which a lot of employers will want so it's a broad-based scheme.'

- 'I've really gained in confidence since I started.'

Other advantages include:

- You'll keep to the routine of the working day – vital if you are to hold down a job when you are offered one.

- You get feedback on your ability to market yourself.

- You can meet different people and socialise.

The disadvantages
- The scheme may not be flexible enough. Check before you start; what happens, for example, if you are offered another job with another employer while you are on a government scheme?

Improving your chances with a scheme
Of course, you could sit at home instead (see Figure 8). But even if you are unemployed, employers like to see that you've spent your time usefully. Going on a training scheme proves you have motivation.

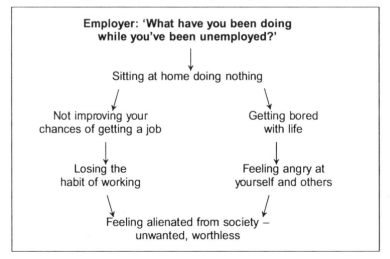

Fig. 8. Facing the consequences of doing nothing at home.

Training schemes can be particularly useful if you have your own special needs. You'll have an intermediary acting on your behalf to help set the placement up – but after that it's down to you. Your attitude to the placement will say a lot about your drive to get your future career going.

Finding out how they assess you
Ask how placement providers help you track the skills and qualities you're developing, and how often. Do they visit regularly or just when there's a problem? Can you talk to somebody currently on the scheme to find out what they think?

Finding out what their success rate is
If you're joining a work experience scheme that should equip you for the job market, why not find out what the percentage is of those who have participated in it and gone on to:

- a job with training
- a job
- a full-time course
- working abroad
- nothing at all.

This may give you an idea as to how effective the programme has been.

Gaining European work experience
The European Union offers the Leonardo da Vinci programme, which in part enables young people in training or going to university to get a placement in a firm in another member state and thereby complete their training. The idea is partly to make sure that you are well prepared for changes in future technology, by learning how to anticipate and cope with change. For more details, see Useful Addresses.

Using your local Jobcentre
You could also contact your local Jobcentre to see if they have a database of vacancies available in Europe.

LOOKING AT YOUR LOCAL COLLEGE OR UNIVERSITY

Employers are increasingly using local colleges and universities to help with training needs. You may find yourself sitting by students who are working four days of the week and attending class on the fifth. You may find you bump into a student who has just come from work to attend class.

Serving the needs of employers

University and college staff increasingly liaise with employers to meet their training and education needs. Consequently, the staff at your local college or university will have their own network of organisations – not necessarily restricted to the UK. International communication links mean that more and more academic and vocational work is being done throughout the world and many more academics have links worldwide. Make use of them!

Shadow a student

If you're thinking of going to university or college, try to arrange to spend a day with a student who is studying the course you want to take. It will give you insight into student life and the course itself. Get help from your careers teacher.

FINDING EXTRA SUPPORT

If you have particular needs, talk through your career thoughts early on with an adviser. This applies to people who need to stay in an area because they have sons or daughters at school at critical stages, as much as it does to those who have particular needs such as people who are disabled in some way, or even those who wish to change career.

Strengthen your position

Get as much experience as you can and keep a close record of what you have achieved, together with references, for the information of future employers. If you are disabled it will help if you can explain to them what adjustments past employers, schools or colleges have had to make to access to buildings, etc, so that prospective firms know what they will need to do, if anything.

Check with your local TEC

There could be programmes in your area targeting people who need some extra help or have specific needs, for example lone parents, people with criminal records, those with disabilities.

GETTING IN TOUCH WITH PROFESSIONAL BODIES

Professional bodies maintain standards. They protect the public from cowboys because they insist that their members provide high quality service and, frequently, that they qualify through a determined route, acquiring specific knowledge defined at national or international level along the way. It is also their job to educate the public about what their careers involve, including the good, bad and ugly aspects of the job.

Getting help from professional bodies

Professional bodies can help you by:

- Sending you information on their career.

- Sending you details of how to train and qualify.

- Providing lists of employers with vacancies or work experience placements (for those at university).

- Attending careers events to promote their careers.

- Putting you in touch with employers in your area who may be able to help.

- Describing skills and qualities you need for their profession.

SUMMARY

- Make use of people willing and able to help you.

- Contact your local TEC or LEC – the range of opportunities may surprise you.

- If you do enrol on a government work experience scheme, go prepared to really learn something and to speak up when you stop learning.

- Review your progress regularly and adjust your training programme as necessary.

CASE STUDIES

John visits his local library

John drifts into the library on Saturday to see what he can find about retail careers. He is nervous and wants to know more about what he will be expected to do. Luckily, the librarian is very helpful. She shows him books on your first job, which has hints about coping with the first day, and also gives him a couple of addresses to write to for more information on careers in retail. Having done some research, John starts to relax.

Susan needs advice on her CV

Susan isn't sure about the way in which you should write a CV so she contacts her local careers company for advice. They give her several examples of ways in which you could construct a CV, and a covering letter, and suggest other people she might like to contact. Susan is reassured.

Mary seeks outside help

Mary is coping well with her new placement. Unfortunately, her husband starts to feel as though she is moving away from him with her new-found confidence and skills. They start to argue a lot, until Mary eventually persuades Rob to go with her for counselling. This helps immensely, and Mary persuades Rob to sign up for a course on his own at night school so that the couple can develop their own interests and share in learning.

6

Making Contact

GETTING PRACTICE IN SELLING YOURSELF

A key ingredient to securing employment is the ability to market yourself to employers. Your efforts to acquire work experience will give you:

- The confidence to sell yourself and blow your own trumpet in future.

- A knowledge of what employers are looking for in the application process.

- Feedback on your own performance.

- Practice in writing a CV and letter of introduction.

- Interview experience.

Your work experience helps, too. It provides you with something to talk about in the selection process in the future.

Jill recruits graduates

Jill recruited graduates for a leisure company's management development programme. The selection process involved an evening dinner, for the company to see how the candidates handled themselves socially and to give the candidates an opportunity to sell themselves.

'Our last dinner was disappointing,' Jill commented. 'Out of six graduates, only three were able to speak about themselves; the others hardly said a word.' So talk.

Tell the company about yourself.
Give them an idea of who you really are.

Having faith in employers
Employers have a vested interest in helping anyone seeking work experience for several reasons, for they can:

- Recruit via work experience placements, knowing that you fit the company well.

- Promote themselves and the careers they offer.

- Contribute to the local community and to the training of the next generation of business leaders, managers and specialists.

- Use students on work experience to train their managers of the future to develop and coach people.

- Keep in touch with educational developments and feed back their thoughts, so helping to prepare the leaders and managers of tomorrow.

- Train the workforce they need for the future.

Identifying ways to make contact
You could contact employers by:

- telephoning – but most will want a CV anyway

- faxing your CV and an introductory letter

- sending an e-mail on the Internet, attaching your CV

- meeting them at careers conventions and sending out a follow-up letter and CV

- meeting those coming in to give talks in school, college or university

- writing a letter

- asking a local government agency or teacher/tutor to make contact for you.

EXPLAINING WHAT YOU WANT AND CAN OFFER

Some employers offer vacation schemes, designed to give you experience, perhaps in your field of study. Your careers service will have details of these, and you should make haste to check them out, because some will be dealt with by employers on a first come, first served basis. Some of the more competitive schemes may have surprisingly early application deadlines.

If you cannot find such a scheme, or do not wish to take part in something so structured, you'll have to hunt for an employer who will give you some experience. In many cases, this may be a matter of either temping for a variety of employers through an agency, or getting a job; or it may be up to you to write directly to employers and ask if they would give you an opportunity to work alongside their employees. Some employers have tasks or a project which need doing, but that nobody else has time for, such as updating a database, writing a computer program, doing research or even organising the office summer/Christmas party. They might simply be glad of an extra pair of hands for a short period of time.

Working out the skills and qualities you have to offer

In Chapter 1 (page 23), you checklisted your life experience so far. Add as many things as you can to that list now, then analyse these activities for skills. Start off by asking yourself exactly what you did as part of the activity and who you dealt with – who were your customers? What skills did you need to do these activities? Stuck for ideas? Here are some examples of skills:

- communicating
- handling difficult people
- juggling several things at once
- working in a team with colleagues
- helping and advising people
- taking accurate orders
- listening to customers
- handling money
- working under pressure
- welcoming and greeting people
- recruiting and supervising staff
- training staff
- planning ahead
- ordering goods from a supplier
- interviewing people
- developing an idea, a design
- writing
- creating something
- managing people, tasks
- co-ordinating a project, or event
- organising something
- promoting things
- fund-raising
- caring for people/pets
- entertaining
- viewing
- identifying something
- studying
- fixing machinery
- selling things
- persuading
- solving problems
- using your initiative
- handling urgent things

- making decisions
- researching
- questioning
- debating
- meeting targets
- teaching others
- negotiating with people
- solving problems

- leading others
- motivating people
- choosing
- counselling
- handling change
- presenting something
- analysing things
- managing your time

Think of those things which you've done; which skills are the most relevant to the sort of work experience you want to do? Emphasise them to show an employer you have what he wants. Even a paper round shows an employer you have:

- commitment – to do it every day
- stickability – whatever the weather, you stick with it
- the ability to go out and get your own job – you're motivated
- reliability and punctuality
- an entrepreneurial spirit
- time management – you can juggle the round with school and the rest of your life.

– so long as you spell these skills and qualities out in your application.

Putting this information in your CV

Any jobs you've had, paid or unpaid, will show an employer that you've got some experience of business life already, and the motivation to go out and get work. Describe the skills and qualities involved in doing them, as in Figure 9. Having outlined these, you can now include them in your letter asking for work experience. Be prepared to give examples, however, to show times when you have exhibited a personal quality and show what this means to others.

For instance, nursery nurse Kerry explained what her punctuality and reliability meant to those who employed her:

'I was always on time for my babysitting evenings. The parents I was sitting for never had to worry about my being late or not showing up, which meant they could look forward to their evening without any hassle.'

IS THIS YOU?

How would your friends describe you? What sorts of adjectives would you use to describe the qualities you need to do the work you've done in the past?

Conscientious	Reliable	Punctual
Clean, tidy	Cheerful	Enthusiastic
Loyal	Innovative	Determined
Shy	Confident	Brash
Quiet	Ambitious	Kind
Sensible	Common sense	Trustworthy
Patient	Tactful	Resourceful
Intelligent	Strong	Motivated
Courageous	Leader	Polite
Compassionate	Intellectual	Critical
Resilient	Sensitive	Friendly

Fig. 9. Giving employers an idea of what you're like.

WRITING THE LETTER

When you write a letter and CV, you're trying to market yourself to an employer and reach the first stage: an interview.

Rules for writing a letter and CV

1. Eliminate any spelling errors.

2. Get your efforts checked by an adviser – listen and take advice.

3. Don't send anything out with stains on such as coke, coffee or chocolate.

4. Most employers prefer that you type your CV or do it on a word processor.

5. Practise writing the letter and CV first before doing your final version.

```
                                          12, Lucky Lane
                                                 Hopeful
                                Always winning 000111BR
                                        Tel: 01234-43210

3 July XXXX

Mrs Twiggle
Personnel Manager
Bank of NewTown
13 Library Street
NewTown NT1 ZZZ

Dear Mrs Twiggle,                                          Explain what you are
                                                           doing
I am currently studying for a General National Vocational
Qualification in Business Studies at Twigglesworth College. I
am due to complete my two-year course there in June XXXX
and am currently considering my career options after that
time.

I spoke to your assistant, Mr Eager, at a recent careers
convention about careers in banking, and he suggested that I    Describe the
contact you. I am very keen to find out more about the          research you've done
opportunities banking has to offer. I read the literature he    so far
gave me at the convention and I have also been in touch
with other clearing banks in the area to find out about their
career possibilities. I would now like to do some relevant
work experience to find out more about the different sorts of   Explain what you
careers available in banking. In particular, I am keen to       want to do
spend some time in different departments to gain a real
understanding of what the various sections have to offer.

I wondered whether it might be possible for me to gain some    Request experience
work experience at the Bank of NewTown this summer             and explain why you
holiday? Your bank particularly appeals because it has local   are contacting them
connections and I was especially excited by the opportunities
you offer students who complete further education courses.

I enclose a CV for your information and would be very          Give method of
pleased to attend an interview. I can be contacted at the      contacting yourself
above number or address; I usually arrive home from college
at about 5pm.

I look forward to hearing from you and thank you for any help  Polite ending
you may be able to give me.

Yours sincerely

Helen Willing
```

Fig. 10. Writing an introductory letter.

CURRICULUM VITAE

Tom Smith
Redwing Cottage, The Bulwarks, Craydon.
Tel: 0111-22222

Career aspirations
To study architecture at university and to become professionally
qualified. Ideally, to work in a French-speaking country.

Education to date
19XX–date   Craydon's Comprehensive School
               Studying for A-levels in Maths, French and
               Physics

19XX–19XX   Craydon's Comprehensive School
               GCSEs achieved in 19XX as follows:

Maths	B
English Lit.	C
English Lang.	C
French	A
Dual Science	A, A
Geography	C
Design & Technology	B

Work experience
Summer 19XX: Sales assistant and petrol attendant, The
             Bulwarks' Garage

- Served wide variety of customers with tact and
  diplomacy; listened to customers' needs and
  responded.
- Handled cash and credit card transactions with
  an eye for detail.
- Able to establish priorities in terms of tasks to do.
- Developed my ability to work under pressure.
- Adhered to health and safety requirements.

Fig. 11. A typical CV.

Autumn 19XX: Work experience at The John Stuart Practice
(Architects)
Two-week placement organised by the school

- Assisted architectural technician with computer aided design, site visits, models, measurements; appreciated need for accuracy and no room for error.
- Attended site visits with architect, also client meetings to observe skills required for handling clients.
- Attended public meeting held to discuss building of new hotel on the sea front; this heightened my appreciation for an architect's talents for tact and persuasion.
- Discovered I could cope with working at great height.

Interests/hobbies

History of building: read history books, visit sites and have put together an album of postcards and photos of my visits and copies from history books on buildings.

Football: Manchester United supporter; play on a local team every Saturday afternoon and train on Wednesday evenings.

Other interests

- Computer literate: Windows 95, spreadsheets, computer aided design.
- Speak conversational French, studying A-level. Spent week in France as part of a French exchange programme.
- Will be taking my driving test in August.
- Date of birth: 9 June 19XX.

Referees

Mr John Williams
Head of Sixth Form
Craydon's Comprehensive School
The Old Hill
Craydon CR1 4JD

Mr John Stuart
The John Stuart Practice
11 Netherton Street
Craydon CR1 2XE

Fig. 11. (continued).

6. Make sure you've got everything you'll need to hand – a record of your results if you have any, your records of achievement.

7. Put your most recent activities first – most employers are interested where you are in your career now, so you need to get their attention.

8. Keep a copy of anything you send out for future reference.

9. Be honest – but don't be bashful, either.

10. Take pride in your work. It's *you* you're talking about.

What should your letter contain?
Figure 10 shows an example of a letter.

PUTTING TOGETHER YOUR CV

The length of a CV is not so important as its content, although many employers prefer CVs that are two pages or less. Keep your CV short, punchy, up-to-date and relevant. Tell employers what you can do for them and give them an idea of what sort of person you are.

What a CV should include
Most CVs will include your:

- name
- address and telephone number (home and university if you are studying away from home)
- date of birth
- marital status and nationality
- educational background
- any work experience – paid and unpaid
- any positions of responsibility
- leisure interests and hobbies and evidence of those
- the names and addresses of two referees.

Take a sheet of paper and jot down the information you would put down about *you*.

What order should information go in?
There are no hard-and-fast rules about this, so play with your CV and practise writing it until you find an order that you feel comfortable with. Common sense dictates that you put your name,

address and telephone number at the top. Most students in full-time education will put their educational history first, because it's what they've done most recently.

Figure 11 gives an example of a typical CV. Note that Tom has mentioned the skills and qualities architects need, such as paying attention to detail, listening to customers' needs and prioritising work. His interest in the history of building demonstrates that he spends his free time looking at different designs and ideas which will improve his creativity in the future. It will also give Tom and the employer something to talk about at interview.

Explaining educational qualifications

Be specific about what your course has covered. Since courses have expanded so much and changed in nature recently, many employers have not kept up-to-date with these changes – for example, BA Media Studies means very little to them. Show how the study skills you've acquired are relevant to an employer.

Including all your work experience

This applies however irrelevant it may appear to you. It will at the very least show your prospective employer that you have self-motivation to go and get yourself work.

Using referees

- Ask your referees if they would be willing to give you a reference before you put their names down.

- Let them know what you're trying to do so that they can comment appropriately.

- Let them know how you got on.

Practise putting your CV together

Have a shot at writing your CV now. Show it to a careers adviser and get advice on the order, they way you have presented it and whether it could be improved. Don't forget to check it for spelling errors.

Sending off your letter and CV

The next step is to post these documents off. Wait up to a week and if you haven't heard anything, call to make sure your letter arrived.

FOLLOWING UP ON YOUR LETTER AND CV

Making a phone call

You could find out what's happening by calling on the pretext of making sure that the employer has received your letter and asking when you might hear something. If you're lucky, you could be put through to someone in charge of the boss's diary.

State clearly why you wrote

The employer could be having a very hectic day and may need a quick reminder from you about who you are and why you wrote. Ask if you could come in for a meeting, if the employer feels he is able to help.

Making your efforts work for you

If the employer cannot help you, don't sulk. There could be lots of good reasons why the firm cannot help you at that time. You can always go back to them later on. Thank them, either by letter or phone, and then ask that vital question which could open other doors for you: 'Can you suggest anyone else in the industry whom I could approach?' For a start, many employers won't want to lose a motivated person to a competitor!

Show you're being tenacious and persistent and your efforts will, somewhere along the line, pay off.

Finding a local professional network to help you

Local professionals may belong to committees and groups for all sorts of reasons. Find a way into them – it will increase your network and it could open a lot of doors. Find out if there's a local chairperson and write to him or her explaining what you want to do.

Is there a firm that's expanding locally?

This is a good time to offer your services and get noticed! Watch the press for articles on local organisations which are expanding due to success. Drop them a line with your request; an extra pair of hands can go a long way, especially if they are willing and motivated!

EXCELLING AT INTERVIEW

If you have prepared well, your interview should be more of a discussion about the placement or job. If you haven't done any preparation, you're more likely to find the employer asking you lots of questions. The company know what they can offer, but they want to find out whether you will fit in well with them and what you can offer. You know what you want because you've worked it out, but you want to know whether the organisation, and the people in it, are right for you. Would you *want* to spend the entire working week with them?

Prepare an explanation about your course

It's important that, if asked, you should be able to give a two or three sentence reply describing your course. Many people fall down at interview because they can't explain their course properly to employers.

Explaining what you want

This will probably be the first opportunity to explain:

- why you want work experience
- what you want to get from it
- what you're looking for
- and to discuss the opportunity further.

Employers will be very impressed that you've given this some thought. Far too many people turn up for interview without doing any prior thinking at all.

Market yourself. You want to show you're serious about this job/placement. So plan ahead.

Practise answering questions

Take advantage of any chance to practise your interviewing skills:

- Ask your school or college to bring in local employers to give your group interview practice.

- Take advice and listen to those who spend time recruiting – they know what makes a successful candidate.

- Read any articles you can in the newspapers about interviewing techniques.

- Read books about successful job hunting.

Try answering these questions

Start thinking about some of the questions you might be asked
during an interview. How would you respond to these, for example:

- Tell me about yourself.

- Why have you approached us? Have you approached anyone else?

- What are your career goals?

- How far have you researched your career plans to date?

- How are you doing in your course?

- Is there anything you feel strongly about?

- What do you think your greatest strengths are?

- Why should we offer you work experience?

- What can you do for us?

- What will you do if we cannot help you?

- Why are you seeking work experience at all? Why not just look
  for a job?

- What do you want to gain from this company?

There are pros and cons of doing preparation, but they are rather
one-sided:

Advantages of preparation
- You'll give the impression of someone who is serious about the
  company and work.

- You'll be able to enter into more of a two-way conversation with
  the interviewer(s).

- You'll be more relaxed if you know you have prepared well.

Disadvantages of preparation
- You may find some unexpected questions a great surprise – be
  ready for those, as interviewers may want to see how you
  respond.

Checking your preparation

Have you: *Done*

- Found out as much as you can about the company?   ....

- Checked the careers library for details about the
  career or area you want to investigate?   ....

- Reminded yourself of what you have to offer?   ....

- Read as much as you can about the training and
  qualifications required?   ....

- Thought of some questions to ask?   ....

- Found out where the interview will be?   ....

- Worked out how long it will take you to get there?   ....

- Decided how you will get there?   ....

- Organised what you are going to wear?   ....

- Checked your clothes are clean, tidy and well pressed? ....

- Polished your shoes?   ....

- Got a hair cut?   ....

You want to look serious about your career, not as if you are applying for a rock group (unless, of course, you're applying for a rock group). Don't overdo the jewellery, makeup and perfume, or outlandish clothes.

Do:

- be polite to everyone you meet however unimportant they may appear

- smile

- thank people who help you in any way

- greet your interviewers with a firm handshake

- ask questions as they occur – an interview should be a two-way discussion

- talk about your achievements – don't hide them

- be honest – you'll get found out if you're not

- make sure your personal hygiene is first class

- have an early night the night before your interview – your brain needs to be fresh

- have a good breakfast, even if you don't feel like it.

Don't
- lie

- swear

- eat sweets or chew gum during your interview

- drink alcohol beforehand – people will smell it on your breath

- lose your temper – if you feel yourself getting under pressure, ask for a minute or two to think about the comment just made, count to ten and take deep breaths

- pick your nose or sniff – take a tissue with you.

Reaching agreement...
If, at the interview, the employer agrees to give you work experience, you will have to do one of two things:

1. You can set your own agenda of things you wish to find out about and then tick them off as you cover them during your work placement experience. Share it with the person who is in charge of you and ask for their help in getting this covered. They may also suggest other things which should be on your list.

2. You could, with your new employer, put a training schedule together prior to your starting the placement. This may help if you want to develop specific skills, for example, or it could be essential if you are embarking on a scheme or programme.

> **Lay out learning objectives and ways of working out how effectively you have covered what you wanted to learn, otherwise the experience could lose some of its potential power.**

I did six months in a bank as a secretary after my typing course, but made no effort to find out about the business or how all the sections pulled together or what they did. I just went in from 9 to 5, took my hour for lunch, typed letters and had a very dull time. Looking back, I wasted a brilliant opportunity to learn how a business functions. I suppose you could say I slept on the job for six months.

Susan, temporary secretary

Let your employer know of potential medical problems
This is for your own sake, as much as anything else. If you have asthma or epilepsy, for example, or any medical conditions which could flare up at work, you must tell the organisation you're doing work experience with and give them the telephone number of people who can be contacted in an emergency.

...and not reaching agreement
If, at the end of the interview when you and the interviewer have found out more about each other, it turns out that the company cannot help you, there are still gains to be had from your efforts:

- You will have had practice and gained confidence in making contact and marketing yourself; get any feedback that you can.

- Find out if the company knows of someone who can help, eg another branch of the organisation or someone they know of in their network.

- You have made contact and could use them in the future.

Whether or not you get a placement (or a job), make sure that you learn from your experience as a whole.

Getting feedback on your performance
Make every interview a learning experience, otherwise they will be a waste of time. Ask for feedback on:

- Your CV and letter of application – how effectively did they sell you?

- Were they clear?

- How did you perform at interview?

- What do you need to work on?

Assessing your performance at interview

When you leave the interview, give yourself time to relax. It's over! Celebrate and then take time to reflect and ask yourself:

- Which bits did I handle well?
- Which bits were awkward? How would I tackle them next time?
- Which questions did I tackle the best?
- How did I cope with meeting strangers?
- How did I handle everyone I met?
- Did I create a good impression?

Write a letter of thanks
Write to thank the interviewer for their time and help, and also anyone else who was particularly helpful and kind to you. It will impress, as many people don't bother.

QUESTIONS AND ANSWERS

Are there any tips for coping with nerves?

Everyone has them – even the interviewer. Put a tissue in your pocket or bag to wipe your hands on if they get wet with perspiration before you go in. Prepare well in advance. Remember that the interviewer wants to get the best out of you, not the worst. Counting to ten also helps if you go blank.

What should I do if I don't know the answer to a question or understand it?

Don't bluff your way. Nobody minds if you don't know the answer and admit it, but if you try to bluff your way through, you'll probably get found out. And if you didn't understand the question, ask for it to be repeated or just say, 'I'm sorry, I don't understand the question'.

What sort of questions should I ask them?

You could ask how many people they have taken on to do work experience before, what they have done and whether they have stayed in touch with the company. You could also take the chance to find out what your hours will be, whether there is a set standard of dress and who you'll be working with. You could also ask the interviewer what he likes about the company, and what prompted him to work there.

Won't I feel intimidated by the interviewer?

Not every interviewer is an expert at interviewing. In fact, many interviewers will have received very little or no training in interview techniques. So be prepared for the unexpected – don't be surprised or unnerved by the interviewer who wanders off on a tangent, waffles, interrupts you, etc. Keep your cool.

SUMMARY

- Take pride in what you have achieved and who you are.
- Market yourself seriously.
- Know what you have to offer so that you can sell yourself to an employer.
- Preparation is a key ingredient to successful interviewing.
- Get feedback at every stage.

CASE STUDIES

John writes to professional bodies
John gets home from the library with his information and composes a letter to the professional body of booksellers. A few days later he is pleased to find they have responded to his request with lots of information. He'd never realised there was so much to working in a bookshop – or that you could reach such a high level of education to do it. He decides to apply for work experience in a local bookshop and is successful.

Susan prepares for interview
Susan is delighted that her letter and CV brings a response from the vet, who calls her in for an interview. Susan turns up promptly, explains that she is considering vet school and brings her current record of achievement. She has talked to her teachers about the grades she is likely to achieve at A-level beforehand, so that she could make sure she has a chance of making vet school. The vet agrees to give her work experience, four days with the vet nurses and one with himself.

Mary identifies another need
Mary has one final area of work experience she wants to try: that of managing staff. She decides to see if she can find a week with an

office manager to shadow her and learn by example. Mary makes contact with an investment bank, whose office manager is very busy but prepared to let Mary follow her for a week. Impressed by the efforts Mary is making to get experience, the bank agrees to let her come for a week ... or longer if she wants.

7

Beginning Your Work Experience

You've got through an initial interview, but there may be a follow-up meeting to:

- Talk to your supervisor.
- See around the buildings to acquaint yourself with people – this can be helpful if you are very nervous about going on work experience.
- Give you a chance to ask any questions you may have before starting.
- Ascertain exactly what you want to get out of your placement.
- Discuss any matters relating to health and safety at work, confidentiality, etc.
- Learn about hours of work, the standard of clothing and behaviour expected.

Give as much thought to this meeting and take as much time over your personal presentation as you did the first time.

LAYING THE GROUNDWORK
Discussing your training
Depending on what you want to do, the employer will probably need to talk to people in his organisation who will be involved in your placement, such as your supervisor or people in different departments. You may need to have a short meeting again, after he has done this, to finalise the placement.

Signing confidentiality agreements
You may be asked to sign a document stating that you will maintain confidentiality and not talk about anything that takes place in the

company while you are on work experience. Don't be surprised or fazed by this form: read it carefully. If you don't understand anything on it, ask about it. Sign it. *Maintain and respect that confidentiality.* If you don't, you're reducing the chances of others to get work placements.

Having a learning contract
You need a learning contract. If there isn't an official contract (unlikely for the shorter work experience), make a commitment with yourself.

What's in a learning contract?
A learning contract could include the kind of information in Figure 12.

Managing the first day
Many people are nervous on their first day. At the very least, you should have the name of someone to report to, who will welcome you and look after you. This may be someone from the personnel office, or in a smaller organisation it could be a secretary or your supervisor.

Let someone at home know where you are
Tell your parents or guardian, partner or flat-mate, where you are going to be, what you'll be doing, the hours you'll be working and how they can reach you in the event of an emergency.

Meeting and greeting others in the company
It can be very nerve-racking, walking down a row of desks or people who are all looking at you, thinking 'who's that?' Take comfort – glances are usually brief, because people need to get on with their work. As you meet your new colleagues:

- Be cheerful - smile! It makes you look confident, even if you are trembling with fear inside.

- Remember that most people want to welcome you to their company – they will remember what it was like to be new and will want to make you feel at home.

- Be polite: don't forget the please, thanks, nice-to-meet-you, thank you for your help. It doesn't cost you anything, and it shows you in a good light.

LEARNING CONTRACT

Company: Biggles' Turbulent Airlines
Date: 18 July – 22 July XXXX
Hours of work: 10.00am – 6.30pm with one hour for lunch
Supervisor: Jay Herald, Personnel Manager
Aims of experience: To find out about careers in the travel industry

What I want to learn:
- Expand my knowledge of where airlines fit into the travel industry
- What careers are available within it?
- What skills are required to work in this industry?

Day-to-day duties:
1. Shadowing employees as listed below
2. Completing diary of information learnt

Method of learning: *Work shadowing*:
- a) Marketing Director
- b) Finance Director
- c) Personnel Director
- d) Chief Operations Manager
- e) Customer care staff – one day with them at ground level
- f) Cabin crew – attend one day training course on safety update

Date of review:
Wednesday, 20 July with Mr Herald at 5.00 for 30 minutes to review progress

Measuring success:
Produce a report for presentation to the group at Monday's staff meeting, outlining:
- Clear role of what each employee on above list does
- Understanding of how they all work together
- What opportunities airlines like this have in the future and what threats they face
- Where I see my skills and interests matching any of those
- Whether I feel the company has goals and direction.

Possible long-term outcomes: Careers implications

Signature: _____   Date: _____
            Rob Brown

Signature: _____   Date: _____
            Jay Herald

Fig. 12. A learning contract.

Finding out those essentials

Many newcomers will automatically get a guided tour to show them where everything is. Sometimes in the hustle and bustle of a working day a phone may ring, a conversation may start and before you know it, you've been forgotten. You may need to make sure you find out a few things.

Checklist for finding things

- Coffee/tea. Find out if you have to pay for these, plus whether you can have as much of it as you like or whether it is restricted. Don't assume goodies like biscuits, etc are there for the taking; you may be taking foodstuffs belonging to a member of staff. Check first.

- A place to hang your coat. Find a cupboard to hang your coat up in. It will keep it looking neat and tidy, and save on cleaning bills.

- The loo. Many people hate asking strangers where the loo is but let's face it, it's an essential.

CHECKING HEALTH, SAFETY AND INSURANCE

Employers are responsible

Employers are legally responsible for visitors who are legally on their premises, including students and teachers, but remember that **you** have a responsibility to obey all health and safety rules. You are responsible for the safety of not only yourself but others around you.

Be safe

When you start work experience, you must know:

- who is in charge of you while you are at work
- whether there is any safety literature you can read
- what your own personal responsibility is for your own health and safety and those of others around you
- who is in charge of first aid and where they are
- whether there are any areas you are forbidden to enter, machinery you cannot work, dangerous substances you must leave well alone.

The workplace can be dangerous. Make sure you don't fall foul of any of these common safety errors:

- loose wires
- locked fire doors
- computers too close to your seat
- disobeying health and safety instructions.

Fire! Fire!
You should be told:

- what the fire alarm sounds like
- where you should go when it goes off
- what to do in the event of discovering fire or if there is an emergency
- who the fire marshall is.

Are you insured?
If you are doing work experience organised by your school or college, the institution normally deals with this matter for you. When you start work experience that you have organised yourself, make sure that you have talked to your company about the issue of insurance. Many employers will have work experience covered already, but you need to make sure that this is the case.

Next of kin
Does someone at work have details of your next of kin (ie your parents or guardian) in case of an accident? They should do.

Looking after yourself
Working is tiring. So make sure you get plenty of rest during your first few days. This means few late nights, relaxing evenings, good food – and a good breakfast! If you're tired, it will be harder to concentrate and do well.

If you're at school or college, remember that the working day is longer than in education. Nor will you get breaks, as a rule. The pressure is on all the time – you have to be on your guard even when discussing what you did the night before, because the phone could ring at any moment with a demanding customer at the other end.

Being assertive
Many employers are appalling at making sure that newcomers and

visitors to the building are shown fire exits, etc. Be polite, but if necessary, as the questions above yourself. 'Can you tell me what the fire alarm sounds like?' etc. Most employees are so used to being at work, that they stop thinking about what they would do in an emergency – and they forget their obligations about health and safety.

HAVING THE RIGHT ATTITUDE

Showing a professional approach

Here are some dos and don'ts to help you:

Do:

- Start and finish all tasks assigned to you.

- Check their deadlines so that you can prioritise your work.

- Check how mail is to be sent out: eg by courier, fax, post, e-mail or bike.

- Watch, listen, learn and ask.

- Keep personal calls to an *absolute minimum.*

- Obey all rules – they are there for health, safety, and confidentiality.

- Get involved in social activities wherever you can.

- Thank people who help you, however small their act of kindness may be.

- Offer to help others under pressure.

- Ask if you don't understand what you are supposed to be doing.

- Adhere to the dress code.

- Ask if you're not sure of what you're doing or supposed to be doing.

- Be friendly.

- Answer the phone if it rings more than three times and no one has picked it up.

- Check your work for mistakes before you hand it back – errors are costly at work.

- Respect those you're working for and learn as much as you can from them.
- Enjoy yourself!

Don't
- Use the phones to organise your social life (even if the staff do).
- Use the photocopier for your personal stuff (even if the staff do).
- Use the fax machine, telephone and e-mail to catch up with friends around the world (even if the staff do).
- 'Borrow' office stationery.
- Try to pick up a date.
- Blame others for past failings you've had.
- Join in gossip about other staff members.
- Lose your temper or swear.
- Smoke, if it's not allowed.
- Spend hours in the loo fixing your hair.
- Not show up – if you cannot make it in, call to say so.
- Leave your desk looking as though it's been hit by a tornado.
- Leave every day bang on the dot of 5 or 5.30 – it looks at if you *hate* it there!

Being enthusiastic
Working isn't terribly interesting and exciting all of the time. You can't expect it to be. Some people want more excitement that others in their work – some employees prefer the routine, others the unexpected. Do the routine tasks diligently and carefully. If you show attention to detail and precision in your work, you are more likely to be entrusted with more challenging things to do. If you can't get even the easy stuff right, how can an organisation be expected to give you anything more demanding?

TRACKING YOUR LEARNING

Keeping a daily diary
Keeping a diary is useful because you'll more easily be able to remember what it is that you've got from your experience. Don't keep one which describes every minute from 9 to 5; instead, keep it short, sharp and meaningful.

Complete the task sheet in Figure 13 to help you build up your knowledge of what you are learning. By the end of your experience, you will have gathered a lot of information about yourself, the

Tasks I have done today: ....

....

Skills I have used: ....

Qualities I have seen used: ....

The skills I enjoyed using the most were: ....

....

What I have learnt about the way in which organisations work and

business is conducted: ....

....

I have handled these situations today: ....

....

How I feel I coped: ....

Fig. 13. A task sheet.

workplace and how you fit in to it. More on assessing this in Chapter 8.

Taking notes at work

Take a notebook and pen to work with you. Make notes, but not of any confidential information. Check with the person you're with that it's okay for you to take notes while they're talking. It puts some people off.

You may find yourself taking notes on:

- what you're learning about the world of work

- what you're learning about different careers

- what you're actually doing so that you have evidence of the things you've done for later on

- thoughts that surprise you.

Advantages of keeping track
- it's easier to remember what you've learnt and done
- it's easier to record your achievements
- you can easily refer to them when applying for jobs
- it makes learning more effective.

Disadvantages of keeping track
- it takes time
- it can be a pain to do at the end of the day when you're tired.

If you're tracking the things you're doing ask yourself if you would want to do them all day or as part of your job. Your accuracy will be very useful for career interviews later on.

Taking responsibility for your development
If you were to reach a point when you're not learning any more, tell someone and do something about it. When you stop learning you become bored and fed up – and you won't be doing work experience any more. You'll be providing cheap labour instead.

If you stop learning, you could:

- Talk to your supervisor about your progress to date – be prepared to support your statement that you need to move on with evidence of things you've done well and areas where you've improved.

- Arrange to talk to your training provider and/or supervisor about the next stage of your training. It could be that you should be looking at moving into full-time employment instead of continuing with that employer, or perhaps you should move to a new employer who can offer training if your present employer can't. That said, you shouldn't walk out just because you've stopped learning. You also have a responsibility to your employer to finish any tasks you've been set. Be flexible.

Meeting with your placement officer/employer
Review your progress regularly, especially if you're on a lengthy placement programme. If you're on a scheme, you should get a review anyway – but it's partly your responsibility to make sure that they happen. If people are busy and haven't come to see you, it's

your job to give them a gentle and polite reminder.

Setting an agenda for the meeting
Put an agenda together and circulate it to those who will be present well before the start. Ask if there are any items anyone wants to add. Your agenda could look something like Figure 14.

Preparing for this review
The more preparation you do, the more you'll get out of the meeting. You shouldn't expect your employer to do some preparation without doing some yourself. Be ready to comment on each item as you go through them. Prepare some questions to ask. Come away with another action plan for your development.

At the end, thank your supervisor for his help and let him know how much you appreciate his support and time. Mention anyone else who's been particularly helpful.

Go prepared to listen
You may not agree with some of the things you are told, but you should be ready to reflect on what you're told. If your work or attitude are criticised, your supervisor should be able to give examples of evidence. Don't be defensive; you're doing work experience to learn from your mistakes. You should, of course, also go with specific examples of what you think you've done *well* and why.

Review meeting with Mandy Biggins
Thursday, 22 May at 10.00

1. General comments

2. Progress to date: please complete attached chart prior to meeting. (You could use the skills charts in Chapters 2 and 8 for you and your employer to go through.)
    – Transferable skills
    – Technical skills and knowledge
    – Working relationships

3. Do any changes need to be made to the placement?

4. Further development

5. Any other business

Fig. 14. Agenda for a review meeting.

STRENGTHENING YOUR NETWORK

Making an effort to meet people
As well as the people you actually work with, you'll have access – depending on the size and nature of the firm – to contact with people as outlined in Figure 15. Make the most of this opportunity – you never know where these contacts could lead.

Networking further
All of these people will have their own network of contacts. They may be able to suggest people who can help you further outside of their organisation.

It is far easier for these people to see what you really can do when you are on work experience than to try to ascertain what you are capable of during a couple of interviews.

Increasing your knowledge
Some of the things you could ask people at work include:

- What advice do you have for people at school/college/university these days?

- How did you get to where you are today?

- What do employers look for in new recruits in . . .?

- How am I doing?

- What do you do? Why? What skills and knowledge do you need to do it? How did you acquire them?

- What is your role in the company?

You can probably get some very useful advice from those who really look as though they've done well and enjoy what they're doing. Target them as your mentors and get their advice. What has made them so successful? How did they find their niche? What would be their advice to you? Reflect on it.

Making an impact
If you work well, fit in and show that you can be part of a team, many bosses will want to do what they can to help you, especially if you ask their advice. If, however, you sulk and whinge, they won't be too impressed and won't want to recommend you to anyone.

Marketing personnel

Catering staff   Auditors

Business development planners

Finance   Accountants

Company secretary

Public relations specialists   Administrators

Information officers/librarians

IT staff   Insurance advisers

Researchers

Managing director/boss   Sales staff

Clerical/secretarial staff

Legal advisers, lawyers   Human resources personnel

Environmental department

Health and safety workers   Union officials

Training department members

Medical staff   Engineers

Fig. 15. Networking on work experience.

COPING IF THINGS GO WRONG

I've just woken up and feel really ill. I don't think I can make it in today. What should I do?

If your placement is on a structured programme, you may have been given guidelines for what to do so check the details first. Otherwise, let your supervisor know. You should also tell them if you've got anything outstanding from the previous day left to do.

I feel so isolated. Everyone is friendly but I just can't seem to make friends.

If you're feeling isolated, try to join in the chat for a few moments over coffee. Ask people about their weekend; if there are photos on their desk of their children, ask about them. Try to start up conversations by asking people about themselves and joining in office activities. Gradually the feeling will go, but it does take time to get to know people.

I've been in my placement for ten days and I'm so bored I could scream or walk out.

If you're constantly finding that you are bored in your work experience placement, there are a number of things you could do. You could:

- check you are really keeping track of what you're learning
- ask if you can move up a level
- ask if you can do something more challenging (only if you're doing what you've been asked to do well)
- talk to your supervisor or the person in charge of your placement
- re-negotiate your placement.

Boredom on any work experience placement usually results from one of three things:

- a desire for more responsibility
- the work or organisation doesn't interest you
- you're not putting any effort into the work experience; you're just turning up.

I can't get on with my supervisor

There will always be people you don't particularly like or are immediately drawn to. You probably didn't like everyone in your class at school, so you can't expect to like every single one of your workmates, but a lot will depend on your attitude and how sociable you are. You could:

- Ignore your dislike and rise above it; the placement won't be for long. Concentrate on doing the job well.

- Move sections, but this won't teach you how to work with people you don't like.

- Talk to someone in the firm about it – perhaps the personnel manager – or a trusted person outside it and ask their advice.

- Talk to the supervisor and see if you can work things out.

Walking away won't achieve anything. Sorting it out one way or another means that you can cope with it when it really does matter and you know you can't leave.

Respecting others' wishes

It may not be possible to take part in or observe everything you want while you are gaining work experience or shadowing someone, especially if the work is confidential and sensitive. If this is the case, respect it as such. For example:

- Some hospital patients may object to you watching medical procedures as they are carried out; others won't mind. The staff should always get a patient's permission for you to be present.

- It may be more difficult to get to spend a lot of time with people in counselling, social work and the legal profession because of the confidentiality and sensitivity of the work.

- You may need to wait until you are older in some areas to gain work experience. Some professional organisations have rules preventing young people from taking part in or observing particular situations.

Dealing with difficulties

Coping with the unwelcome will give you confidence. There will always be times when things aren't going well, but they are those you remember most and even laugh at later on. You put it down to experience. Dealing with unpleasant situations will give you confidence because you've handled it and know you can cope again. That's why work experience will build your confidence, even though it may not feel like that at the time.

Feeling it was awful

A negative work experience placement can have positive outcomes. If you were desperate to follow a career, but you didn't enjoy your work experience and decided it wasn't for you, so much the better. You found out early on, before investing time and money in training. Work experience will soon show the trouble spots of most careers and give you a chance to decide whether you will be able to cope with them. Just watch the reactions of those working in the business around you!

Advantages of sticking with it
You will:

- learn how to stick with it and keep going until the task is done – vital when things get tough

- learn about another business

- gain confidence

- be able to handle a similar situation with greater ability the next time.

- impress.

but:

- it could be uncomfortable for a while – like a bumpy flight.

SUMMARY

- It's your responsibility to speak up if you're not getting the experience you wanted.

- Make sure you respect the Health and Safety at Work Act.

- If things go wrong, don't walk out. Try to sort things out – you'll learn far more from the experience.

CASE STUDIES

John gets the taste of work

John settles in well to the bookshop. He remembers the school's advice: 'Keep busy, keep smiling and always ask if you need help'. He hardly notices when it is lunch time. The staff there are very interested in him and friendly. He talks to his supervisor about retail careers in bookselling. 'Don't limit your options,' she tells him, to his surprise. 'Look at other careers involving information too, like librarianship. Do some more research.'

Susan demonstrates her commitment

Susan turns up at her work experience full of enthusiasm. She offers her services for the very dirtiest jobs, does extra hours, helps out wherever she can and talks to the nurses about their work. The staff are impressed and ask if she would like to come back at Christmas. Susan has won the respect of the professionals she is working with by showing that she cares for all the animals she works with, and their owners, and isn't afraid to get down to the harder, dirtier work. She also sees the application of subjects she is doing at school, such as biology and chemistry, and goes back to her studies determined to work well.

Mary gets down to work

Mary arrives full of enthusiasm. She goes to meetings with the office manager, and she sees first-hand how the office manager deals with her responsibilities. Mary is always cheerful, offers to help with any tasks no matter how menial, and develops a fine set of skills and proves she has personal qualities which make her a natural fit in the organisation. At the end of Mary's second week, she is the subject of discussion at a management meeting: they don't want to let Mary go! How can they keep her?

8

Assessing Your Learning

This chapter will help you assess what you have learnt from work experience. You can use parts of it, too, if you have done voluntary, paid or casual work, or held positions of responsibility.

DECIDING IF THIS CAREER IS FOR YOU

In Chapter 2 (page 30) you had a list of possible questions to ask about careers you were investigating. You now need to follow that up.

Getting up to date

Make sure that the information you have gleaned from your research with people at work is current. There are now far more ways 'in' than previously. For many occupations, the career path has completely disappeared and the traditional inflexible methods of training have given way to more flexibility, opening up access through all sorts of routes. Some sources of information are:

- *Occupations* (see Further Reading)
- the professional body of the occupation
- your careers service
- the Internet.

Checking the facts against yourself

You can do this by answering the following questions:

Questions to ask people at work and professional bodies:	Questions to ask yourself:
How long does it take to qualify?	Are you prepared to spend that length of time training?
What sort of exams are needed to enter training, eg A-levels/ GNVQs, GCSEs, degree?	Are you going to be able to meet those requirements? Will they be too easy to reach and should you

	be aiming higher, or too difficult and should you set your sights lower?
What sort of personal qualities do you need for the work?	Do you have them? How can you show that you have them?
Who are your customers?	Can you see yourself working with those sorts of people, eg elderly, sick, rich clients, families?
What's the best thing about being a...?	Does that excite you? Bore you?
What's the worst thing about being a...?	Could you handle that?
What hours are you expected to work?	Does that meet your personal needs?
What does the job/career involve doing in any one working day?	Does that appeal and interest you?
Are there any restrictions which make it difficult for individuals to get into that field, eg colour vision, height, age?	Do any of these relate to you?
What scope is there for setting up your own business?	Could you see yourself doing that?
How is the work stressful?	Could you handle this?
How can you best prepare for this line of work: work experience, evidence of interest needed by professionals?	Are you willing to make the effort?
What other careers are related to this line of work?	Do they interest you (but find out about them first)?
What is happening in the sector locally, nationally, internationally?	Do these issues interest you? Do you have an opinion on them?
What else could you do after training for this line of work?	Does it appeal? If you are made redundant, are there any other options available to you?

Is it a growth industry/career area?	If not, does it bother you? Are you prepared to take the risk? What else can you do to increase your chances of being employed?
What other factors affect its growth?	Where can you find out about these?
How much are you likely to earn?	How important is this to you *vs* job satisfaction?

Taking the next step
Talk through your options with:

- Your trusted careers adviser.

- Friends, family, those who know you and preferably who have experience of the workplace.

- Your tutors/teachers if you are in further education, to check that your goals are within your capabilities and to work out strategies for achieving them if you're not doing so already.

Also check out any related careers which may appeal. Don't rule them out! You could be astonished and relieved that you did cross-check 'families' of careers and find one that was more suitable than you had thought.

Proving yourself
If you want to enter a particular profession, you're likely to need to spend some time proving your interest first to professionals in the field. More experience may be expected of you in careers where entry is very competitive and training costly. Persistence usually pays off – and make the most of any opportunity you can to network.

Learning more by moving
If you go back to the same firm for further work experience make sure you're doing different tasks, expanding your CV and skill base.

Advantages of going back
- It proves your commitment and interest.

- You know everyone so it's less stressful than starting somewhere new.

Disadvantages of going back

- You could be stuck doing the same job. Talk to your supervisor or the personnel manager to make sure this doesn't happen.

- You could be putting all your eggs in the same basket – so make sure you network with other companies.

Experience with different sorts of companies will help you to:

- compare small and large businesses and find which best suits you

- compare private as opposed to public organisations

- get a flavour for a different sort of work

- further your skills

- network and improve your chances of getting a job by making yourself known to more companies.

LOOKING FOR THE ORGANISATION THAT FEELS RIGHT

Every organisation is different. Some feel more 'you' than others. You'll spend a lot of time at work, so it's worth asking yourself some serious questions following your work experience. For each question:

– think about the organisation you spent time in

– ask yourself how you felt about that

– ask yourself how important that element of company culture is to you. For example, size will be more important to some people than others.

Looking at the company you went to

- How large was it?

- How did it measure success?

- Was it international?

- Was it formal or informal?

- Was it open plan or did everyone have an office to themselves?

- How much did the management dictate to staff or consult them?

- Did you have to clock in and out?
- What age group was the staff?
- Was it a family business?
- Did each individual have to set their own targets annually?
- Did the company reward individuals and/or teams for good performance?
- Did you have to wear a uniform?
- Did it involve much travelling time to work?
- Was it organised or chaotic?
- How social was it?
- Did the firm look after employees well?
- Were office politics rife?
- Was the organisation committed to staff training and career development?
- Is it the sort of place I could look forward to working in?
- Does the firm respond to change or create it?

Answers to questions like these will give you an idea of the sort of organisation you're looking for and what's important to you at work.

Get up to date on the sector you'd like to work in
Do some background reading – this is especially important if you're graduating and moving into a graduate role. Find out who the main players are and where companies stand in the FTSE. Look out for news items about the sector, its main players, mergers, acquisitions, successes and failures. Try to get a feel for the trends in the sector, and the strengths, weaknesses, threats and opportunities facing it and those companies in it.

Refer to your research throughout your application. Show you're interested and that you read the papers and keep up-to-date with world events and the business world. Be able to talk about things that are particularly relevant, newsworthy or controversial. Have an opinion and be able to support it.

Look at the company you've worked for and then at yourself. How do you match up?

BUILDING A PICTURE OF THE WORKPLACE

Think about the way a business or organisation functions by looking at the places you've done work experience in. How do you relate to it? Can you apply situations you've been in to those you might see in business?

1. *What does the organisation do and why does it exist?*
Does this interest you and would you want to work for a company with similar goals?

2. *What are its goals?*
Do those excite you and would you want to participate in achieving those sorts of goals?

3. *Who are the main customers?*
What sort of customers do you want to serve? For example, people with social problems, sick, on holiday, needing a service at home?

4. *What does the organisation do to keep its customers and acquire new ones?*
What did you have to do to reach a goal you had?

5. *How does it seek to improve its service?*
Are you continually looking to improve the way things are done? Give an example. Suggest ways the company might improve its service.

6. *What emphasis is placed on staff training and career development?*
What difference would that make to you as a member of staff, and as a customer?

7. *How do they promote their goods and services?*
What other methods could they use? Is there anything you've promoted yourself recently? What was the result?

8. *What makes a quality product?*
Give an example of something you've done particularly well. How would this relate to something you've seen in the workplace?

9. *How does the company eliminate waste in terms of money and time?*
Give an example of something you've done to save or budget for. Look for ways of controlling a budget without spoiling the overall product.

10. *What sort of hierarchy is there?*
What effect could this have on your career? What sort of level do you want to be at?

11. *How do staff contribute to the future of the organisation?*
Do you contribute for example at school/college by sitting on committees, getting up petitions? Do you do something about things you feel strongly about?

12. *How much responsibility is devolved to each member of staff?*
How much responsibility do you want to have in your future career? Do you want to lead others or be led?

13. *What responsibilities does a manager have?*
What has happened to the role of managers in the last 20 years? Would it interest you? How do you become a manager?

14. *How is the business structured?*
Check what individual departments do – would any of them appeal to you?

15. *How do colleagues ensure they are all heading in the right direction?*
How do companies communicate to staff? How do staff react? What steps must a leader or manager take to enthuse staff about change, goals, direction and dealing with problems/pressures?

16. *What pressures is the business under and how is it responding?*
How do you cope under pressure? Look at ways to cope.

17. *How are staff recruited?*
What can you learn from the ways they have joined?

18. *Who are the leading companies in this line of business?*
Would any of them appeal to you as a prospective employer?

19. *How does the organisation communicate internally between staff, and externally with its customers and suppliers?*
What means of communication are used? What do staff have to think about when communicating with each other and those outside the organisation?

20. *Who is it accountable to? How does it have to show accountability?*
Who does the top management report to? How often do they do this
and by what means? What happens if their goals are met? And if
they aren't?

Looking at what you've learnt
Some of your reactions to your new-found knowledge about the
workplace may have surprised you, but you should have learnt a lot
about the way an organisation works. Work experience enables you
to comment on issues affecting businesses and understand the
workplace better.

Take the chance to learn more about people
Look at your co-workers closely. What motivates them? Can you
spot the nine-to-fivers, who watch the clock and are clearly there just
for the pay packet or those who are passionate about the business
and what they're doing? How do they differ in their approach to
work and their enjoyment of it? Who is reaping the greatest
rewards? And how closely do those rewards match your own life
expectations?

ASSESSING LIFE AT THE TOP

To get an idea of what it's like at the top, or at least close to it, and
decide if it's for you, find out:

- What does a leader do?

- How much contact does he have with his staff?

- To whom is he responsible?

- What is his background likely to have been?

- What has he done to get to where he is today?

- Where does he see himself going next?

- How far does the boss get involved in the local community?

Finding out about the skills and qualities needed
What qualities have you seen managers and leaders use? You may be
surprised by some of them. A good knowledge of current
international affairs is probably one of them.

Look at yourself. Can you think of times when you have:

- led others
- taken charge
- taken early responsibility and wanted more
- taken risks?

Take advantage any time you can to practise your skills in leading others and to build up confidence.

Get feedback from the rest of the team on your performance and what they thought of your leadership. Think about what you did well, badly and how you would do things differently next time.

MEETING COURSE REQUIREMENTS

Seek advice where you need it

If you've got a project to do on which you'll be assessed, don't leave your work until the last minute. Get going on it so that you can sort out any problems or uncertainties as they arise and not the day before your work is due. If you feel as though you're getting snowed under, talk to someone and come up with solutions to tackle the problem.

Get concrete facts from your tutor and work in conjunction with your employer and tutor to ensure that you're going along the right lines to meet the course criteria. Think about:

- Which subjects are going to be particularly important for your career?

- What standards will you need to achieve to get to where you want to be?

- Has your experience given you any ideas for any projects, etc that are necessary for your course?

- How have you used the study skills you need at school or college in the workplace?

- Are there any subjects you need to put more work into, perhaps because they are your weaker ones?

EVALUATING YOUR SKILLS AND QUALITIES

Assessing your basic skills

The basic skills you used in your work experience were probably: communicating in writing, communicating verbally, numeracy, information technology and learning.

- What forms of written and verbal communications did you use, e.g. letters, faxes, e-mail, telephone, face-to-face discussions? What did you learn about communicating at work?

- How did you use your numerical skills, e.g. for accounting, balance sheets, billing, percentages?

- Did you make any presentations, or see any? What did they teach you about the range of materials used to present material, the language the presenter used and the environment?

- What IT have you use, for example, Word, Powerpoint, Excel, Outlook, Lotus Notes, databases, the Internet? Make a note of what you used IT for and how you used it. Be able to specify which systems you used.

- How quickly were you able to pick things up and get to grips with the environment you were in and what was going on?

- How could you develop/improve your skills further?

Assessing your transferable skills

You completed this chart in Chapter 2; now it's time to assess how you've used your skills on work experience so that you can compare the two and see how you've moved on.

1. Tick the box you think reflects how well you used the following skills while you were at work. For each one, you should be able to give an example of how you used the skill.

2. Ask a supervisor or manager to complete the box in terms of how they see your skills. Can they help you improve them?

3. Compare notes. Find out why they ticked what they did. You will gain a clearer idea of how others view the way you handle yourself and how you use your skills.

	Very good	Quite good	Average	Not good	Poor
Anticipating and adapting to change					
Working as a team					
Leading others					
Planning and organisation					
Establishing priorities					
Allocating resources					
Setting goals					
Meeting targets					
Analysing information					
Making decisions					
Solving problems					
Customer service					
Business awareness					
Negotiating					
Presenting material					

4. Which ones would you:
   a) like to improve?
   b) like to use most at work?

5. Now look back to all the jobs and positions of responsibility you've had. Analyse those for the skills listed above, and you'll be in a far better position to promote this experience on your CV.

Setting targets for yourself

It helps to discuss your overall performance with someone, either in education or school. If you need to seek ways to improve your transferable skills and knowledge base, discuss how this can be done at work. If you set targets for yourself, you're more likely to work hard to achieve them because they are yours. Decide what feels right for you.

Some employers place greater emphasis on some transferable skills than others. It depends on the role employees have and the sort of organisation they work in. The ability to deal with a wide range of people effectively is, however, a vital one.

Coping with sudden changes and demands

Work experience gives you the chance to see how you react to change and the unexpected. Think back to something which happened that was unexpected during your placement. How did you react?

Work experience gives you the chance to see how you handle change and the unexpected.

During your time on work experience, what changed for:

- The company as a whole?
- Current events in the UK?
- The team you were working with?
- You and your life?
- Your relationship with those you live with?

Can you describe a situation where you deal with something which happened unexpectedly or meant urgent action was needed? How did you deal with it and those around you?

Life is full of changes

Take a major change you've experienced in your life. It could be moving house, changing school, going to university, having children. What changed for you and how did you cope with that change?

Noting the personal qualities you used

Which of the personal qualities you had did you need to use most while you were at work? Think of a situation you could describe to an employer where you had to use them. For example, tact in dealing with a rude customer, patience in listening to a customer's needs, persuasion when making your case. If you enjoy using these qualities you might want to make use of them regularly in a job. For example, if you enjoy helping people you could:

1. Do voluntary work where you can use your caring qualities outside the workplace, perhaps at weekends or in the evening.

2. Use your caring qualities in a career where you need them all the time.

3. Put them to good use in customer service.

How hungry are you?

Are you determined to:

- be successful?
- be an achiever?
- get things done?
- be competitive?

How do you think these qualities relate to the workplace and how far did you see these goals displayed by individuals at work? Can you feel this drive and motivation in yourself, or are you a gentler sort of person, perhaps seeking to use your caring qualities?

Look back at those qualities you had developed in Chapter 6. Can you think of examples of how you needed them and used them at work?

MEETING YOUR AIMS

Was your work experience placement effective? Ask yourself:

- How far were my aims met?

- How much did I learn about myself while finding a placement and then on work experience?

- How helpful will the experience be in finding paid employment?

- How much confidence have I gained?
- What difference will this experience make to my future and my career planning?
- What is my next step?

Resolving any unsatisfactory bits
Decide how you can complete those. This could be done by a couple of days' extra work experience, specifically working on those areas you didn't complete, or perhaps a phone call to get the information you wanted.

Assessing what you contributed to the organisation
- What did your work contribute to the overall goals of the organisation and to the section or department you were in?
- What did you personally bring to the company?
- What difference did you make being there?
- What were you appreciated for? (work and personally)
- Did you save others time, money, energy?
- Did you contribute new ideas, a different approach, solutions to problems?

Employers love people who question the method of doing something, especially if they've been doing it the same way for a long time.

Many employers find a fresh pair of eyes very refreshing.

'There's nothing like having someone stand over your shoulder, saying "Why do you do that?" Many times, you find yourself asking why you *are* doing it. It certainly sharpens you up.'

Manager

MAKING CONTACTS LAST

Write a thank you letter
You should also enclose your CV, if you want to work with the

organisation. Ask about the possibility of future work, full- or part-time, paid or unpaid.

Visit
Keep in touch with them. Drop in for a quick cup of coffee and a chat.

Be social
Meet them for a drink at their local wine bar to catch up with them. Even if there's no vacancy at their firm, the staff may bump into somebody they know working for another firm which could use your skills.

Network
If you know of someone you think would be interested in working for the company (even if you're not), connect them with it. Many companies take people on by word of mouth – it saves them a lot of time and hassle.

SUMMARY

- Assess and evaluate your activities as you go to increase the effectiveness of what you're learning.

- The more open-minded you are, the more you will learn.

- Keep a record of what you've learnt in a file or folder to refer to when you apply for jobs or courses.

- Be prepared to share your new-found knowledge with others and discuss it.

CASE STUDIES

John starts seriously researching his career
John returns to school with greater enthusiasm for his career. His eyes have been opened to careers he hadn't thought of. He talks through his options with his careers adviser and then changes his A-levels to give him a basis for applying to courses involving information science.

Susan widens her experience
Susan has followed up her experience with the vet's practice by visiting as many places involving animals as she can. She talks to

anyone involved in animal care about furthering her experience and knowledge to make sure that, of them all, veterinary science is for her. She keeps a diary of all her efforts to give to her headteacher, who will complete her reference for university.

Mary learns about herself

Mary finishes her two weeks with the company. When comparing all her placements, she realises how much she enjoyed the office manager role, ensuring that the office ran smoothly and looking after the employees to ensure their needs were met. That, she thinks, is the sort of role she is looking for.

9

Putting Your Experience to Work

FIRST STEPS FIRST: RESEARCH

So, you've said goodbye to all your new friends at work and life has returned to normal. What's next? Well, you need to use your experience to take your career forward.

If you're job hunting, get out there and approach employers
- Apply using the traditional 'response to adverts' approach; or

- Create your own job by writing to employers who might want the skills, knowledge and personal qualities you have.

Do your research
A key ingredient to successful job hunting is research. Yes, this takes time and effort, but *the candidate who has done her homework stands out from the crowd.* The further up the education ladder you are, the more you'll have to do. A graduate would be expected to do more research about the company, the sector and business life, than a 16-year-old school leaver. At graduate level, you'd be expected to do background reading about the sector, talk to people working in the industry, visit different employers, read trade magazines and keep up-to-date with current affairs – especially those affecting the sector. Research shows that you know what you're letting yourself in for.

Find out about the company and where it's going
Read the company's brochures, visit its showroom or branches, find out what sorts of products it sells, who its customers are and whether you'd want to work with them, how large it is, etc. Talk to people working there to get the real insider story. Get an idea of the basics: for example, if you were applying for a job as a hotel receptionist, you should read a copy of the hotel's brochure so that you can show that you're aware of the facilities if offers by talking about them at the interview. If that hotel is part of a larger group, it

would be helpful to have read the group brochure, too. It shows interest, and you'll get a better feel for the organisation you're seeking to join.

Find out about the job if it's advertised
Go to your local careers library and find out about the work you'd be doing. Talk to people doing a similar job, if you can. Find out about what the job involves, the skills required, the qualifications required and the training available. If you think the job looks interesting and the industry excites you, apply. The evidence that you have the skills they require need not come from the workplace; look to extra curricular activities and your educational achievements for evidence.

ANALYSING AN EMPLOYER'S NEEDS

Know yourself
You need to know where your career interests lie (many employers will ask how you planned your career), what you want out of a job, the sort of organisation you'd feel comfortable in (large or small for example) and to have a vision of where you want to be in, say five years' time.

Compare yourself against the job
Checklist your skills, qualifications and experience against the ones the employer wants. This is where relevant experience makes it much easier to sell yourself convincingly. If you have most of the skills, qualifications and experience they're looking for, apply.

Think about what the employer wants
Let's take an example. If you were applying for a job as a tour guide, it wouldn't be sufficient to talk about your travel experiences as a backpacker. You must show that you can handle the job and the people you'll meet, and that you have the skills and qualities the job will demand, such as:

- the ability to think calmly under pressure and to handle emergency situations

- organising abilities

- the ability to relate to a wide variety of people

- a good general knowledge of the country you're going to guide in

- the ability to represent the company running the tours in such a way that the customers on the tour will travel with them again

- stamina and grit, a sense of humour, a positive approach and patience.

Half the battle in getting an employer to notice you is showing that you've actually thought about what the work might entail and that you have the skills and abilities required to do it. When listing your work experience, highlight particularly the skills you used which an employer would need in the position you're applying for. If you were writing directly to an employer to see if she would be able to offer you a job, you would need to highlight those skills you specifically want to use at work.

Look at the work you want to do

Think about your own position, now. You may have seen a job in the paper, or on the careers service board, which appeals, or you might want to write to a company and offer your skills on the off-chance they might employ you. Try completing the following:

The content of this work is likely to involve:

_____

_____

_____

The skills I need to do this job are:

_____

_____

_____

The qualities I need to do this work are:

_____

_____

_____

> **Look back at your part-time, Saturday and holiday jobs.**
> **Include them in your application.**

Don't tell yourself or other employers 'I've only done this,' or 'I haven't done anything, really.' Even 'just a Saturday job' is useful experience.

Checklist your experience to date and analyse it carefully for:

- the skills you have to offer – look back to pages 80 and 123 for examples of skills you might have used at work

- your willingness to learn

- your ability to handle change, identify and solve problems, and to use your initiative

- what you've learnt about yourself, business and commerce, and how organisations work.

Consider how the above are relevant to your prospective employer. You will have lots of opportunity to promote them in:

- your CV
- the application form, if there is one
- your covering letter enclosing your CV/application form
- the interview.

Use examples of things you've done as part of a job or an aspect of your life to answer questions on application forms such as, 'Tell us about a problem you've encountered and how you overcame it', or 'Describe a situation when you worked in a team to solve a difficulty. You should say something about your role.'

> **Show an employer the link between your skills and their needs.**
> **You'll make yourself stand out from everybody else and increase**
> **their interest in you.**

Think 'transferable skills'

You can use your transferable skills from other sectors or other jobs to show that you have the experience necessary to do the work.

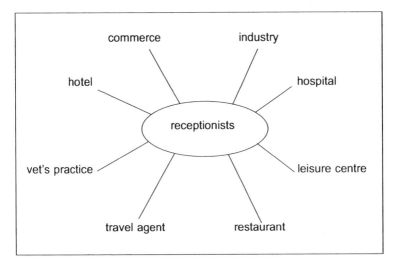

Fig. 16. Transferring skills from one company to another.

Making your experience work for you

Let's assume you've seen an advert for a trainee travel agent, perhaps calling for someone with 'experience of travel'. Travel stories alone won't grab the attention of the interviewer. Think about the skills a travel agent will need: IT abilities, customer care, selling skills, an ability to work under pressure... and then on your CV or application form *show* the employer that you have developed these skills as follows.

If you've worked in a shop on a Saturday, you'll have developed relevant skills, which can be entered on your CV as follows:

Work experience

Summer XXXX **SuperFood Supermarket – Check-out operator**

Responsibilities included:

– dealing with customers at check-out and helping them pack their goods in a friendly and efficient way
– handling money accurately and honestly (cash, credit cards, cheques, direct debit cards)
– working under pressure at peak times
– being a reliable and punctual team member of the check-out staff

This doesn't cover IT abilities, so you could look for evidence elsewhere that you have these by:

- talking about any IT experience you've had at work, in an education setting, or at home

- listing the skills you do have to date and any qualifications you have in this area.

Under hobbies and interests, you might put your travel experiences and expand these to describe the sort of travel you've done and the skills and qualities you needed to do it.

Hobbies and interests:

> **Travel**: Went inter-railing in Europe (Summer, 19XX); visited 18 cities in 27 days so became adept at seeing a lot of a city in a short space of time.

Highlight your transferable skills so that an employer will instantly see their relevance to what they want. Never assume the employer will know that your skills are relevant.

PROMOTING YOUR EXPERIENCE – SOME EXAMPLES

Spell out to an employer what you can do

Here's the selling bit. Don't just put the name of the employer you were with and the title of the job you did:

Summer 1998   Harold, Martin and Pain Dental Surgery
               Dental receptionist.

This tells the employer very little, so show him what your experience involved and about the skills you've acquired, as Figure 15 shows.

This receptionist has highlighted the skills she has developed through her responsibilities.

Going for the more senior post
If you were applying for a more senior position than that of

Summer 19XX   Harold, Martin and Pain Dental Surgery
                Dental Receptionist

My responsibilities included:

Customer care: welcoming patients, answering the telephone, making appointments and assisting with patient care. This needed tact and sensitivity, with a friendly, warm approach. Attention to personal presentation and hygiene was important.

Administration: filing records, sending out appointment cards, making up bills and sending them out; attention to detail was important.

Managing my time and **working well within a small close team.**

Handling emergency situations and **working calmly under pressure.**

Fig. 17. Outlining skills gained during work experience.

receptionist – say a trainee management position – a shortened version would show that you understand the importance of:

- quality customer service
- maintaining records
- teamwork.

You could put something like:

Summer 1998 Harold, Martin and Pain Dental Surgery
Dental receptionist – Six weeks

Tasks involved welcoming and assisting the general public, maintaining office records and bills and supporting the three dentists in the surgery. These:

- Taught me the importance of teamwork, office management and quality customer service to ensure that a business runs smoothly.

- Gave me a useful insight into how a small business is run and the problems it faces.

This candidate has chosen to focus on what he has learnt about what makes a business operate well, while showing that he developed some specific skills in handling people, supporting colleagues and being able to deal with more routine aspects of the workplace.

Interviewers will expand on your CV at the interview
Both versions give the interviewer and candidate something to talk about at the interview; for the more senior candidate, the interviewer might ask the candidate to expand on the statements he has made, so some background reading by the candidate to show he has done further research would be useful.

Use facts and figures where you can throughout your application
These support your statements and provide evidence that you can do what you say you can – just as you would in an essay.

'Answered 300 phone calls in the first two hours after the lines opened on the first day the company offered this new deal. I can work calmly under pressure.'

'Answered the telephone.'

The first line gives them some idea of how you coped with the pressure on the first day and what you've had to handle. Line two merely says you did a task.

Talk about what you've done at the interview
Here's an example Tom described at an interview, thanks to his summer job at a bank:

'Over my three month period with the bank I wrote a report of 30 pages outlining the services available to students and how they compare. I presented it to the four members of the Marketing Team which decides on the future strategy for business development. They accepted three out of my four suggestions.'

Tom
Economics student
Summer scheme with bank

Tom gave his prospective employers a good idea of:

- what he achieved within a given time
- the level the report was presented to
- how effective his work was
- the skills he developed in researching, analysing and presenting material.

Compare his statement to Alice's:

> 'I wrote a report and gave it to my superior. I don't know what happened to it.'
>
> Alice
> Economics student
> Summer scheme with bank

This tells you little (or a lot) about Alice's abilities, drive or motivation. Didn't she care what happened to her report?

Include examples of your experience, skills and abilities throughout your application
- Think of examples of each skill to tell interviewers about – problems you solved, customer complaints you had to handle, situations you had to negotiate your way through.

- Describe projects you've worked on which are relevant to the company you're applying to in terms of the skills and knowledge you needed.

- Remember all you've achieved, the people you worked with, the things you saw and did at work, the situations you handled. Use them to demonstrate you have the skills required for the work in hand.

Preparing for the interview
Plan well for the interview by re-reading your application and thinking of questions you might be asked.

Try answering some of these questions
Many interviewers ask similar questions, and you can usually depend on the following being covered, so work out how you would answer them yourself.

- Tell us about yourself.
- What are your career goals? Where do you want to be in five or ten years' time?
- What are your strengths?
- What are your weaknesses/areas for development?
- Why should we recruit you over anybody else?
- What can you do for us?
- Why are you applying to our company?
- Tell us how you planned your career so far?
- Why do you want this job?
- What do you know about our company?

You might also be asked about statement you've made on your CV, in an application form, or in your covering letter. Prepare examples to demonstrate your abilities and skills in advance.

Take time to respond to questions
There will be many things you can talk about in an interview as a result of your work experience, so when you're asked a question about situations you've faced or dealt with, take a deep breath and think about your answer before responding. Think back through your past experience to look for the best example to answer the question. Don't fear the silence – work with it. And question your interviewers: an interview is a two-way process. Ask about training, staff development and the job itself to show that you take your career and the organisation seriously. Those referring to holidays and perks display a rather less thoughtful approach.

Any selector will be interested in skills you can offer
In particular, they will welcome evidence that you can:

- plan your workload and focus on tasks to be done
- manage your time
- find a balance of work and social life
- make a contribution to the organisation
- take advantage of the opportunities offered to you
- work with minimum supervision
- plan your career and self-development
- research and analyse information
- communicate well with a wide variety of people
- work well in a team.

Outline the skills and qualities you have acquired when applying for a course

If you are applying for a vocational course, then your work experience will be of considerable interest to the selectors – in fact, they will expect you to have done a great deal of investigating into your chosen career wherever possible. Comment on the research you've done and how your experience has contributed to your decision to study the course you're applying for.

COPING WITH GAPS IN YOUR APPLICATION

Be honest with yourself

If you lack most of the skills, qualifications and experience listed in a job description (particularly those described as important or essential), then you should re-think and look for another job. But if you have most of them, you should ask yourself the following questions.

Is there likely to be a perfect candidate?

It is extremely unlikely that one candidate will have every single thing the selector is looking for. Even if he did, there's still the 'fit' within the team to be considered. Most selector will draw up a wish list of things they hope candidates will bring to the job under different categories often reflected in the advertisement.

Wish list	Ways it might be reflected in a job advert
Essential	Applicants must have Previous experience in this area essential
Important	Applicants should have A . . . is important
Nice to have	Would be useful Would be helpful

Develop strategies for dealing with the areas you're lacking

You will strengthen your chances of getting the job you want if you can develop a strategy for lacking any particular skills or strength: for example, you could:

- show that you're willing to train and learn

- use any experience you have in a voluntary capacity which is relevant to the job in hand.

Think broadly

Remember that not all of these examples need be taken directly from the workplace. Describing instances when you've used specific skills outside work – say in a voluntary capacity will help cover any gaps in your workplace experience.

Interviewer: John, can you describe a time when you've lead a team through a project?

John: (John stops to think. He hasn't led a team at work, so he looks to his extra curricular activities to show he has the abilities the interviewer is interested in.)
At university I was in charge of organising rag week in our department. The main challenge was making sure that our antics weren't frowned upon by the locals – many thought students were just a noisy bunch. At the same time, I had a very enthusiastic team bursting with ideas – most of them very public and very loud. It wasn't easy trying to get a balance between the two – but we managed, and we raised over £3,000 for charity in seven days.

John has given the interviewers some indication that he has:

1. led a team
2. taken the views of all parties into account
3. been aware of local implications
4. harnessed the goodwill of his team.

The interviewer might pick up on any of these aspects of leadership with follow-up questions and even, perhaps, what John's ideas of a good leader are.

LOOKING BACK

Applying for a job is an experience in itself, so learn from it. You'll quickly get a feeling for those questions you handled well, and those aspects of an interview you feel less comfortable with and need to work on. Some organisations will give feedback about an application performance, but try to evaluate your performance yourself as well, perhaps by talking it through with a careers adviser. Build on your abilities – the following chapter shows way you can do this.

SUMMARY

1. Research should play an important part as you prepare to apply for a job.

2. Use your experience to promote the skills you have to offer and spell out clearly what you can do – don't assume an employer will know.

3. During the interview bring out the skills you listed on your CV and application form.

CASE STUDIES

John puts university and employment together
John wanted greater insight into careers in information science. Aided by his careers teacher, he set up different opportunities to investigate careers in information science. By the time he applied to university, John knew much more about his ambitions, the courses available, and what he would need to do to increase his chances of getting a job afterwards. In his application form, he described the careers research he'd done to date. His research paid off: he got four out of five offers.

Susan gains further experience
Susan kept in touch with the practice which had given her work experience during that first week. During her university holidays, she got more experience by making contact through her previous practice with a vet in the wilder, more rural parts of Britain to give her a different view on vet work. This extended Susan's network and gave her an insight into a contrasting practice.

Mary gets a job and trains further
Mary was offered a job with the investment bank. They asked if she

would be willing to take on some of the more mundane jobs the current Office Manager had to do which freed her up for various projects. Mary accepted instantly and started work. She soon took on responsibility for all the secretarial staff to ensure that things ran smoothly and became increasingly interested in working in the human resources department of the bank.

10

Strengthening Your Experience

ENHANCING YOUR EMPLOYABILITY

Building on the experience of life you've acquired can be done both at work and in your spare time, and enable you to:

- increase your confidence

- practice skills in a 'safe' environment

- give you the chance to try out a possible new career in your spare time

- develop skills you need to give you a better chance in the job market or for promotion at work

- extend your network of contacts

- give you something extra of interest to add to any applications you make.

As well as the workplace, clubs, societies, community organisations and charities, hobbies and interests all give you an excellent opportunity to expand your experience.

USING YOUR HOBBIES AND INTERESTS

Hobbies and interests give an employer an idea of the sort of person you are. If an employer wants a team-minded player, for example, he may look for evidence of interest in team activities under your hobbies and interests.

Hobbies and interests show that you're a well-rounded person
Employers like people who do things other than work and your hobbies and interests show what sort of person you are. They need well-rounded people will fit well into a team to create well-motivated teams who achieve results.

Use your hobbies/interests to provide evidence of personal qualities and skills

The following is an example. Which of the following would apply to someone who studies for and passes music exams? Circle those you think are relevant:

Have motivation	Like to meet standards set by others
Like facing a challenge	Can perform under pressure
Set themselves target to achieve	Appreciate music
Like to spend time alone getting on with their practice	Show commitment

Now think about the line of work you're most interested in. Which one personal quality or ability that you need when you enjoy your hobbies and interests would be of *most* use to an employer in that area?

Analyse your skills further
Take an activity you've done recently:

Activity:_____

Which of the skills listed below did you use to carry out this activity? (You might also want to refer to the list of skills on page 80 to see if you can get extra ideas.)

Collecting	Classifying	Researching
Interviewing	Advising	Informing
Planning	Budgeting	Organising
Negotiating	Creating	Designing
Listening	Selling	Persuading others
Investing	Representing	Showing
Understanding	Influencing	Initiating
Debating	Changing	Challenging
Administering	Promoting	Placating
Directing	Producing	Teaching
Writing	Communicating	Fund-raising
Liaising	Managing	Presenting
Other		

Taking on positions of responsibility
Many people state on their CV that they are members of committees, organisations and groups. Questioned in the interview, it turns out that they don't actually *do* anything other than take the quarterly magazine, or pay the annual subscription.

Clubs and associations can provide an excellent opportunity for you to:

1. Prove your interest in and commitment to a given field (such as animal welfare, child welfare, tourism, engineering, accountancy... the list is endless, especially if you are at college or university); and

2. to develop skills you could use now and in the future at work and promote throughout the application process.

Look to the future and develop skills to meet your needs
You might have visions of working in management in a few years' time, in which case any experience you can acquire in supervising and managing people and projects will be very useful, for example, chairing a committee or a group. If you want to develop skills in fund-raising, involve yourself in a group aiming to raise money, so that you can build up your experience.

Skills are relevant to course of a non-vocational nature, too
Provide evidence of your interest in your chosen job or course, and your application will carry far more weight. If you were going to study history, for example, your evidence might consist of:

- visiting historical sites, museums and plays
- participating in the local history society if there is one near your home
- taking advantage of various archaeological digs
- reading around your subject outside of class (so that you can mention specific historical periods you favour).

VOLUNTEERING

Getting involved in the community
Many people want to put something back into the community, and

they get involved with a variety of projects, such as:

- working as a volunteer for English Heritage at a site
- teaching adults to read, spell and do simple arithmetic
- acting as advisers to Young Enterprise companies
- sitting on local committees or councils
- offering help to clubs for young people with behavioural problems
- visiting the elderly and doing simple jobs for them.

Activities such as these can be invaluable in career planning because things happen when you volunteer:

1. Voluntary work can be a very effective way to develop skills you need for a particular role at work you might want, such as supervising others, counselling people, raising money and organising an event. Many organisations run training programmes for their volunteers

2. Your confidence will increase and show through in all areas of your life.

3. Your ability to work with a very wide range of people will improve as your communication skills and interpersonal skills develop.

4. You get a great feeling of personal satisfaction and sense of worth, because you are putting something back and helping others.

5. Your voluntary efforts may lead to another career, either:
   - working for a charity after you've retired from business life, so that the charity can benefit from your skills, experience, business contacts and knowledge; or
   - moving from voluntary work to doing it as a job. Many professions want to recruit people with experience of life.

'I started to do a couple of hours a week to help people with their English at the local college. I loved helping people learn to read, or improve their reading. After a while, I wanted to get more involved in teaching English. A tutor at the college told me about a course designed to qualify you in a few weeks. I enrolled, got a career development loan, and am now teaching English to people at the local college. Next year, I might go abroad – Spain, perhaps...'

Suki
Teaches English

TAKING RESPONSIBILITY FOR YOUR FUTURE

Be an active learner and expand your experience

You can keep learning at work by taking on a project outside your job description. Why not sit on a committee with a role so that you get to know people in different departments and raise your profile while fine-tuning your skills? Or see if your company can arrange a secondment in another part of the organisation?

Many people groan at the thought of taking on a sideways move in the organisation ('Why move and have all the hassle, unless I get more money?' is a typical response), but this can be a great way to build up your experience *and* build up your profile within the organisation. Coaching and training others can be a useful way to build up your skills in motivating and developing other members of staff – useful qualities in any manager.

> **Make a commitment – your CV should look different every year. Vow to yourself that yours will.**

ADDING TO YOUR EMPLOYABILITY

Build up your knowledge

If you're particularly interested in a career area, become an expert in that area by building up your knowledge about it. There are various ways you can do this:

Devote time to learning about the sector you work in
Use the media to keep informed of current events and development which could affect your company or line of business. You can then spot:

- companies which you could target in terms of offering your skills and knowledge

- what is happening to the industry – whether it is growing or declining

- the global and European factors affecting it

- new products

- what it takes to be successful and a cut above the rest.

Network with people within the sector
Take time to make, nurture and foster contacts you have in your line of business – and outside them. Treat them well, do things socially as well as in business – and your network will last. You never know, it could also land you with that great job, contract or opportunity.

Be able to show what you have achieved
- Make sure you can describe your achievements effectively – in and out of work.

- Set yourself targets.

- Be proud of what you achieve.

- Look to improve your performance and that of the company.

- Seek to excel in all you do.

- Watch what your competitors are doing. You could end up joining them.

SUMMARY

- Track and develop your skills, strengths and weaknesses throughout your education and working life; it will pay dividends.

- Make learning a life-long commitment.

- Watch the job market all the time – learn about it and what it has to offer.

- Anything you can take on which will increase your confidence for the future in your own abilities and widen your network of contacts will benefit you. You never know where a chance meeting might lead.

CASE STUDIES

John develops his transferable skills

John makes good use of his days at university. He gets a part-time job, working in a student bar, and gains a good deal of experience in the summer working for a local company who put his theory of information science to good use. John's parents encourage him to use his careers service early on, but John's own efforts pay off – the local company he had experience with over the summer offer him a job.

Susan finds her niche

Susan is glad that she's done some work placements with a vet on the wild side – she decides that she prefers to work in a town practice and seeks employment. She enjoys the variety of animals and people she works with – but knows that her early experiences have taught her that she likes to work with smaller animals most of the time.

Mary moves into human resources

Mary enjoys her work with the secretarial staff. She takes on more and more responsibility for them, and meets with the office manager to talk about her extra work. Mary suggests that some of her routine tasks might be delegated to the secretaries themselves, enabling them to develop. Mary enrolls on a course leading to a professional qualification in recruitment. She's found her niche.

Glossary

Action planning. Setting out a number of things you need to do; effective with deadlines and targets.

Assertive. Asking for what you want and speaking your mind without being aggressive and making the other person feel inferior.

Attitude. How you approach life and your responsibilities.

Block release. Released from college for a block of two or three weeks to gain work experience in industry; or, where you are released from the workplace for two or three weeks to attend college.

Career planning. Planning your career and making sure you have the skills, qualifications and attitude to get you to where you want to be.

Company culture. The atmosphere within a company, how it sees success, what makes the staff happy.

Computer literacy. Ability to use computers and apply your knowledge to work situations.

Core skills. Essential skills that everyone needs – ability to communicate well, both orally and on paper, to work with numbers, to handle information technology and apply it.

CV/Curriculum vitae. Document outlining those parts of your life history that are relevant to an employer, in particular your qualifications and work history.

Day release. A system involving release for one day a week from work to attend college to study for vocationally relevant qualifications and courses.

Feedback. Information given to you explaining where you did well and where your performance needs to be improved.

Gap year. Also known as a year out. A gap between secondary and further education, or further and higher education.

Goals. Setting yourself targets.

GNVQ, General National Vocational Qualification. Studied at a college of further education or sixth form. Many offer a work experience placement.

HND/C, Higher National Diploma/Certificate. A vocational qualification which may encompass work experience.

JobClubs. Help unemployed people to find work through offering them access to facilities such as a computer to write up a CV and letter of application, a telephone, sessions on how to find a job and general advice.

LECs, Local Enterprise Councils. Scotland's equivalent to TECs in England and Wales.

Life-long learning. Essential to surviving in the workplace today, if you want to be employed throughout your working life. Knowledge becomes outdated very quickly.

Modern apprenticeship. The commitment by a young person and an employer to a training agreement which describes the training, work experience and qualifications that young person will be working towards on an Apprenticeship scheme.

Networking. A chain of contacts or information – you can network with computers as well as people. A network of contacts gives you lots of access to all sorts of information.

Numeracy. Ability to work with numbers and use them to analyse information, carry out basic calculations, handle figures, gather and process data.

NVQ, National Vocational Qualification. Obtained in the workplace by assessment in realistic work situations.

Personal qualities. Special to *you*. Adjectives your friends or family might use to describe you.

Professional bodies. Organisations which set the standard for their area in education, training, behaviour and professionalism.

Recruitment agencies. Private firms involved in finding employers the right person for a vacancy; also help individuals find the right job for them.

Secondment. A period away from your normal work, perhaps within another organisation or a different branch or office of your current company, designed to provide you with specific learning opportunities and build experience to further your career.

Skills. Particular abilities which can be used directly in the workplace, such as in numeracy, information technology, organisation and planning.

Strategy. A careful planning of the way forward to reach goals.

TECs, Training and Enterprise Councils. Local companies created to enhance economic growth and employment opportunities in the area. They work with other agencies in the region involved in employment and training.

Temping. Short assignments of paid work, usually found by signing up with a recruitment agency, which can give you a broad insight into lots of different organisations and careers.

Transferable skills. Skills that are used in many different jobs and will travel or transfer with you from one position to another.

Voluntary work. Work done without pay – or sometimes with accommodation, food and pocket money provided – to help those who need extra support.

Work shadowing. Following someone around at work and watching what they do – literally acting as their shadow.

Year out. See **Gap year**.

Further Reading

DIRECTORIES OF EMPLOYERS

Dun and Bradstreet Business Registers. Available in your local library, list all those companies within a geographical area and their line of work.

Kompass (Read Information Services, annually). The authority on British industry.

Market Surveys (Key Note Limited). Available in your local library. Reports on the state of various sectors in commerce.

The Times 1000 (Times Books, 1997).

CAREERS BOOKS

Graduate Employment and Training Guide (CRAC), published annually. (See Useful Addresses).

Occupations (Careers Occupations and Information Centre), published annually, also available at your local library.

The Training and Enterprise Directory (Kogan Page Limited, 1997).

The 1999 What Colour is Your Parachute?, Richard Nelson Bolles (Ten Speed Press). A very useful book to help you plan your career.

What Do Graduates Do?, The Association of Graduate and Careers Advisory Services (CRAC, Hobsons Publishing Plc), published annually.

INFORMATION ON PROGRAMMES AT HOME AND ABROAD

A Year Off . . . A Year On? (CRAC, Hobsons Publishing Plc). Details of year out opportunities.

Directory of Jobs and Careers Abroad, Vacation Traineeships for Students, Directory of Summer Jobs in Britain, Directory of Summer Jobs Abroad, Directory of Jobs and Careers Abroad, all available from Vacation Work, 9 Park End Street, Oxford OX1 1HJ.

Directory of Volunteering and Employment Opportunities, Jan Brownfoot and Frances Wilks (Page Bros, Norwich, 1995).

Guides to Stages: An introduction to work experience in Europe for students and graduates, J.A. Goodman (CSU Limited, 1996).

Volunteer Work Abroad; *Working Holidays*; *A Year Between*; *Study Holidays*; *Workplace: The complete guide to work experience and work placements*, all published by The Central Bureau for Educational Visits and Exchanges, Seymour Mews House, Seymour Mews, London WC1H 9PE.

SPONSORSHIP

Sponsorships Offered to Students by Employers and Professional Bodies for First Degrees, BTEC and SCOTVEC Higher Awards or Comparable Courses, (Careers and Occupational Information Centre, available from PO Box 348, Bristol BS99 7FE).

Sponsorship and Training Opportunities in Engineering, (Institute of Mechanical Engineers, Northgate Avenue, Bury St Edmunds, Suffolk IP32 6BN).

The Sponsorship Year Book and Sponsorship Insights, (Hollis Directories Ltd, Contact House, Lower Hampton Road, Sunbury, Middlesex TW16 5HQ).

Useful Addresses

AIESEC (Association Internationale des Etudiants en Science Economiques et Commerciales). Assists business and economics students promote contacts between students and employers for jobs and sandwich placements. UK address: 29–31 Cowper Street, London EC2A 4AP. Branches throughout the UK; contact their London address to find your nearest.

Careers Company, local. Check *Yellow Pages*, local telephone book.

Careers Research and Advisory Centre (CRAC), Sheraton House, Castle Park, Cambridge CB3 0AX. Tel: (01223) 460277. Runs Insight into Management Courses.

Community Services Volunteers, 237 Pentonville Road, London N1 9NJ. Tel: (020) 7278 6601.

The Federation of Recruitment and Employment Services Ltd (FRES), 36/38 Mortimer Street, London W1N 7RB. For a small fee, they will provide you with a list of recruitment agencies for finding work in the EU.

GAP Activity Projects, GAP House, 44 Queen's Road, Reading, Berkshire RG1 4BB. Tel: (0118) 9594914. Arranges work experience overseas for 18- to 19-year olds who are taking a year out between completing further education and starting a higher education course.

Kibbutz Reps, 1A Accommodation Road, Golders Green, London NW11. Tel: (0181) 4589 9235. For people aged 18 to 32.

Leonardo da Vinci Vocational Training Programme. For information contact the Central Bureau Vocational Education and Training Programmes, 10 Spring Gardens, London SW1A 2BN. Tel: (020) 7389 4389.

LiveWIRE, Freepost NT805, Newcastle Upon Tyne NE1 1BR. Tel: (0345) 573252 (local call charge). Relevant to 16–26 year olds who wish to start their own business. Offers information and a range of services to help.

Modern Apprenticeships, Return to Work Programmes, etc. Contact your local careers company/service or your local TEC.

Prospects: www.prospects.csu.ak.uk Lots of information here on opportunities for university students, including the Work Experience Bank.

Shell Technology Enterprise Programme (STEP), 344–354 Gray's Inn Road, London WC1X 8BP. Tel (020) 7713 5252.

TEC, your local. Check *Yellow Pages*, telephone directory.

The Year in Industry, University of Manchester, Simon Building, Oxford Road, Manchester M13 9PL.

Index